MOHALLA SETHIAN

"From Ancestors To Heirs : A Legacy Unfolds"

RAJIV SETHI

BLUEROSE PUBLISHERS
India | U.K.

Copyright © Rajiv Sethi 2025

All rights reserved by author. No part of this publication may be reproduced, stored in a retrieval system or transmitted in any form or by any means, electronic, mechanical, photocopying, recording or otherwise, without the prior permission of the author. Although every precaution has been taken to verify the accuracy of the information contained herein, the publisher assumes no responsibility for any errors or omissions. No liability is assumed for damages that may result from the use of information contained within.

BlueRose Publishers takes no responsibility for any damages, losses, or liabilities that may arise from the use or misuse of the information, products, or services provided in this publication.

For permissions requests or inquiries regarding this publication, please contact:

BLUEROSE PUBLISHERS
www.BlueRoseONE.com
info@bluerosepublishers.com
+91 8882 898 898
+4407342408967

ISBN: 978-93-7018-053-6

Cover Design: Aman Sharma
Typesetting: Pooja Sharma

First Edition: April 2025

MOHALLA SETHIAN

THE SETHIS

A Tribute to my Ancestors and an effort to instil pride in the descendants of our ancestors and bring them closer to each other.

DEDICATION

This book is dedicated to my Dear Father, late Shri Narendra Nath Sethi, who dreamed of compiling our family tree. Though his untimely passing at a young age prevented him from completing this vision, he was able to document the first four generations.

It is also dedicated to my Dear Mother, Saroj Sethi, whose unwavering faith in me gave me the strength and determination to fulfil my father's dream and complete this project.

DISCLAIMER

This family history is based on narratives shared by family members, friends, and, where necessary, supplemented by information from publicly available sources.

While every effort has been made to ensure accuracy, some details may be influenced by personal recollections and interpretations.

This work is not intended as a definitive historical record but rather as a tribute to our family's legacy.

Rajiv Sethi

PREFACE

Embarking on a journey to trace my family tree has been an incredibly fulfilling experience. It all began around 1995 when my wife, Kiran, stumbled upon an age-worn piece of paper in my father's handwriting. This fragile, yellowed sheet listed the names of four generations of his ancestors. That simple discovery sparked a deep curiosity within me, compelling me to delve further into my family's history and bring our lineage up to date for the present generation.

The first step in my quest was reaching out to relatives—some of whom I had never met—to gather more information. This proved to be the most rewarding part of the journey, as it allowed me to connect with distant family members, cousins, nieces, and nephews, all of whom were eager to contribute to this endeavour. Their enthusiasm and willingness to share their own family histories led to the creation of the first official version of *The Sethi Family Tree* in 2005, spanning ten generations. The document was shared with family members, who received it with great interest. Over time, as more information surfaced, the tree continued to expand and now, as of today, encompasses an impressive thirteen generations.

While I initially believed my work to be complete, a casual conversation in 2017 rekindled my curiosity. Someone mentioned the name of my clan—*Khukhrain*—a term that sounded both familiar and enigmatic. Intrigued, I turned to the internet to learn more. What began as a simple search soon transformed into an in-depth exploration of my ancestors, their origins, and their legacy.

Through my research, I traced the roots of the Sethi family to the historic town of Bhera in present-day Pakistan. Over centuries, various factors—including economic opportunities, political unrest, and the desire for a better future—prompted my ancestors to migrate from Bhera to different parts of the world. Yet, no matter how far they travelled, they carried with them the values, traditions, and customs passed down through generations, ensuring that their heritage remained intact. This migration was more than just a physical relocation; it was a cultural transformation that bridged the past and the present.

For those who arrived in India before and after the Partition of 1947, the transition was fraught with hardships. They faced immense challenges as they struggled to rebuild their lives in a new land. Yet, through sheer resilience and determination, they persevered—taking on whatever work was available, establishing themselves, and ultimately laying the foundation for future generations. Their strength and adaptability not only ensured their survival but also helped them thrive, becoming ambassadors of their culture while embracing the diversity of their new communities.

As I delved deeper into my family's history, I was filled with a profound sense of pride and belonging. Learning about the sacrifices and struggles of my ancestors made me appreciate the legacy they had built and instilled in me a strong desire to preserve their stories for future generations.

During my research, I also came across families with the *Sethi* surname who remained across the border in Pakistan. Despite being separated for over seven decades, it was fascinating to discover the many cultural traditions and rituals we still shared—an enduring testament to our common heritage. Each new discovery enriched my understanding of the intricate and vibrant tapestry of my family's past.

The idea of turning this research into a book was inspired by a conversation with my children. When I shared my findings with them, my daughter excitedly suggested that compiling these stories into a book would be a wonderful way to document and celebrate our lineage. Her enthusiasm gave me the final push I needed to embark on this endeavour.

This book is a tribute to the rich and enthralling history of the Sethi family. It is my hope that it serves as a valuable record for future generations, preserving the experiences, traditions, and resilience that define our family's journey.

This labour of love is more than just a family tree—it is a chronicle of resilience, migration, and unity. I hope that through these pages, future generations will find inspiration in the legacy of the Sethis and take pride in the history that binds us all.

The title "Mohalla Sethian" is derived from the various Mohallas (areas or neighbourhoods) that were named after the Khukhrain clan, which once dominated certain parts of a town with their grand havelis and estates. These areas, where the Sethi family had their havelis, became known as Mohalla Sethian. Such neighbourhoods were prominent in cities like Lahore, Rawalpindi, Bhera, Sargodha, Peshawar, and other towns now part of Pakistan. Many of these Mohallas still exist today, particularly in Peshawar, where the havelis of the Sethis have been restored by the local government and are being showcased as tourist attractions, highlighted in videos on platforms like YouTube, due to their intricate architectural designs.

It was in one of these "Mohalla Sethian" that our forefathers once lived, within their magnificent havelis. Given that this book chronicles the history of 13 generations of my Sethi family, the title "Mohalla Sethian" is a fitting tribute to the rich legacy and heritage of our ancestors.

Rajiv Sethi

ACKNOWLEDGEMENTS

I am deeply grateful to the many Sethis -- both near and far - who contributed invaluable information and supported this effort.

My heartfelt thanks go to my cousins Kanchan Madan, Sudhir Anand, and Anil Sethi, whose insights were instrumental in shaping this book. My sincere thanks to my nephew, Sanjeev Kumar (Winnie) who helped compile many historical facts about the family. My niece, Amita Sethi Ghai, played a crucial role by organizing a family gathering that proved to be both informative and inspiring and got me in touch with much of my extended family.

I am indebted to my wife, Kiran, whose unwavering encouragement kept me going, and to my children, Anubhav and Aanchal, along with their spouses, Namita and Nitesh, and my grandson, Reyankh, for their constant support and enthusiasm throughout this journey.

A special note of gratitude goes to Ms. Wajeeha Sethi, a professor in Peshawar, whose research provided invaluable information on the Sethis of the pre-Partition era. Her ancestors, along with hundreds of other Sethi families, migrated from Bhera to Peshawar in the early to mid-1800s. Though they converted to Islam, they retained the *Sethi* surname and, to this day, continue to observe many traditions common to all Sethis. Her contributions, including the '*Vanshavali*' (genealogical records) of the Khukhrain clan and historical photographs, have been an invaluable addition to this book.

CONTENTS

CHAPTER 1: THE PLACE OF ORIGIN OF SETHIS – 'BHERA' 1
    BHERA – THE TOWN ON THE RIVER 2

CHAPTER 2- THE SETHI CLAN "KHUKHRAINS" 12
    KHUKRAIN – THE WARRIOR CLAN 13

CHAPTER 3- THE "SETHI" TITLE – MEANING and HISTORY 18
    THE SETHIS – A BRIEF HISTORY 19

CHAPTER 4- OUR ANCESTORS 23
    OUR ANCESTORS 24

CHAPTER 5- THE FAMILY IN PRESENT TIMES 27
    MY FAMILY – FIRST 6 GENERATIONS 28
    SEVENTH GENERATION 30
    EIGHTH GENERATION 32
    NINTH GENERATION 46
    TENTH, ELEVENTH, TWELFTH and THIRTEENTH GENERATIONS 77

The complete family tree can be accessed through the link below:

https://www.familyecho.com/?p=GH6A1&c=3nh31rfdfmddmyxf&f=429069403503030623&lang=en

CHAPTER 1

THE PLACE OF ORIGIN OF SETHIS – 'BHERA'

BHERA – THE TOWN ON THE RIVER

The name **"Bhera"** is believed to have originated from **"Bahu-Rah"**, meaning "multiple roads," due to the many routes that led to the town. Another interpretation traces its roots to the Sanskrit term **"Bhav-Hara,"** meaning "that which dispels fear," symbolizing a place of safety and protection.

Bhera has long been the ancestral home of the **Khukhrain** ethnic group, whose origins can be traced to the Salt Range. The Khukhrains are a distinct set of clans within the **Khatri** caste, traditionally numbered at eight: **Kohli, Sahni, Sabharwal, Suri, Sethi, Bhasin, Anand, and Chadha.** Over time, this group expanded to include more clans. These warrior lineages bore the brunt of repeated invasions on Bhera, defending their homeland against various aggressors.

It is said that **Porus (Purushottama),** the legendary king of the Puru tribe who valiantly confronted **Alexander the Great,** was himself a Khukhrain. Porus ruled over the lands between the **Hydaspes (Jhelum) and Acesines (Chenab) rivers.** The Greek historian **Arrian** mentions the palace of **Sopeithes**, supposedly located on the Hydaspes—believed to be in Bhera.

A thriving and prosperous kingdom, **Bhera** served as a major junction for multiple trade routes leading to diverse destinations. One prominent route extended to the **valley of Kashmir**, while another passed through the **Indian plains** toward **Pataliputra** in the southeast. A third route led southward to the flourishing kingdom of **Multan.**

Bhera - referred to in ancient times as **Bheda**—is believed to have existed since at least **400 BCE**. Throughout history, it has witnessed numerous invasions and upheavals. During the **Battle of Bhatia** in the early **11th century**, the forces of **Mahmud of Ghazni** defeated **Biji Rai,** the ruler of Bhera, and ransacked the town.

In the **13th century CE**, Bhera once again faced devastation, this time at the hands of the **Mongols**. Following the **Battle of the Indus** near **Sojhanda** (in present-day Attock District), **Genghis Khan** dispatched detachments in pursuit of the fleeing **Jalaluddin of Khwarazm**. One of these forces, led by **General Turtai**, attacked and destroyed Bhera before continuing its rampage toward Multan.

In **February 1519**, the Mughal Emperor **Babur** launched his first expedition across the Indus. Captivated by Bhera's fertile and wealthy lands, he seized the city and held it for nearly a month, exacting a heavy ransom. In his famous autobiography, **Tuzk-e-Babri**, Babur describes his ambitions for Hindustan and explicitly mentions **Bhera and Khushab** as part of his territorial conquests. The city, unable to resist the might of the Mughal forces, paid a staggering sum of **two lakh rupees** to secure its safety from plunder.

Two decades later, in **1540**, after defeating Humayun's Mughal army at **Kannauj**, **Sher Shah Suri** pursued the fleeing forces and halted near Bhera. It was during this period that he established the **new town of Bhera** near **Khushab**. Under the reign of **Akbar**, this newly founded settlement became the **headquarters of one of the subdivisions of the Subah of Lahore.**

The new town was built near a site associated with **Pir Kaya Nath**, a revered holy man. His **Samadhi (memorial shrine)** still stands today, along with remnants of the **historic Tirath Sthan (pilgrimage site).** Devotees continue to visit his resting place, and a local family residing beside the shrine diligently maintains its upkeep.

Samadhi of Pir Kaya Nath, Bhera

As was common in those days, Bhera was established within a fortified enclosure, surrounded by towering walls and approximately eight gates, probably rebuilt around 1865 by the British. Few of these structures remain today, and those that do are rapidly falling into ruin due to neglect and disregard for heritage. Some of the gates were named after major cities in the direction they faced - such as Lahori, Kashmiri, Multani, Chinioti, and Kabuli, while others, like Peeranwala and Haji Gulab, were named for unique local reasons. Much of the city's historical architecture has been lost to modern construction, and many of its older communities have disappeared over time.

Mohalla Sethian

Within Bhera's walls lay a labyrinth of interconnected *mohallas* and *abadis*. Each *Mohalla* had its own distinct characteristics and was inhabited by different castes and was often named after the caste that resided there.

Some of the well-known *mohallas* included Mohalla Piracha, Mohalla Sheikhanwala, Mohalla Sahinianwala, Mohalla Khawajgan, Mohalla Kolianwala, and Mohalla Sethian.

Over time, these boundaries became less significant. Traditionally, Bhera's people did not marry outside their clans while living in their ancestral homes. However, after the migration of 1947, when they dispersed across India and the world, these customs gradually faded.

As regards Mohalla Sethian, Bhera still has two '*Sethian Da Mohalla*', '*Vadda Sethia da Mohalla*' that starts from '*Jethu di Khuee*' and the other '*Chhota Sethian da Mohalla*',, that takes off near Kacheri Bazaar and terminates near circular road close to the pre-partition era Ram Leeta Grounds.

The *mohallas* were dotted with grand *havelis* featuring exquisite wooden arches, intricately carved balconies, and elaborately designed doors, often cantered around large courtyards and outhouses. Some of the carved wooden doors in Bhera are now in the Lahore Museum. The carving is both floral and geometric. The wooden balconies or '*Jharokas*' too are a sight to behold.

Over the decades, many families converted to either Islam or Sikhism while retaining their ancestral surnames. Until Partition, *Khukhrains* of all faiths coexisted peacefully in Bhera, a harmony reflected in the city's closely intertwined neighbourhoods. The people proudly referred to themselves as *'Bherochis'* - the proud residents of Bhera.

In the centre of the town was a gurdwara with a tower providing a panoramic view of the city, also referred to as the *"Eiffel Tower of Bhera"*. The Gurdwara is a beautiful quasi-Italian structure. From its magnificent tower, one can see the hills of the Salt Range and the surrounding countryside with its mustard fields and orange and kinnow mandarin orchards.

The Gurdwara of Bhera – Now an Imambargah

The Gurdwara Tower

The Gurdwara of Bhera

Adjacent to the gurdwara was a bustling bazaar known for its finely crafted wooden objects, quilts, and '*khussas*', as well as traditional delicacies like '*pheonian*', *pateesa*, and '*warrian*' - spice balls used in curry preparation. Following the migration of Sikhs from Bhera in 1947, their place of worship was repurposed into an *imambargah* now known as '*Markazi Imam Bargah*'

While the building's layout was altered to reflect its new religious function, several elements of its original architecture remain preserved on both the interior and the exterior of the building.

About a kilometre northwest of Bhera, just outside the town near the Jhelum River, stands the Baoli Wala Temple. Despite its name, no traces of a *baoli* (stepwell) remain. It is believed that flooding from the river may have washed it away, or perhaps a stepwell once existed but was lost over time.

The temple was built approximately two decades before independence by the Chopra family, who were known to be wealthy landowners. However, little else is known about them.

Situated in an open, unoccupied space, the temple has fallen into ruin, possibly due to neglect and lack of preservation.

Another significant Hindu religious site in Bhera, known as the '*Marhi of Bhera*,' still stands today, though few visitors come here anymore.

Once, a deep well surrounded by a dense palm grove was a striking feature of the site. Blindfolded bulls (*kohlu kay bael*) would move in circles, drawing water from the well, while priests conducted religious ceremonies nearby.

The renowned writer Bhisham Sahni rekindled interest in this forgotten heritage through his novel '*Mayyadas Ki Marhi*,' which was set in Bhera and brought the site back into public memory.

Baoli wala or Chopra Temple

The palm grove and the well at Marhi of Bhera.

Bhera boasts the presence of six temples scattered across various Mohallas or neighbourhoods. Among these, three temples are visible only in the ruined state, while other three still stand, but have begun to crumble die to the passage of time.

Nagianwala or Shiva Temple

Another Hindu temple resides in Nagianwala Mohalla, dedicated to Lord Shiva, the Hindu God of destruction, revered by yogis for '*ego*'.

The presence of these temples stands as a poignant reminder of Bhera's historic past. Despite the ravages of time, the temples remain testaments to the town's rich cultural history, urging authorities and enthusiasts to consider preservation efforts to ensure their enduring legacy. Interestingly. the responsibility for the preservation of these monuments falls primarily on the shoulders of a retired army office, Col. (Retd) Zahid Mumtaz, who has taken it upon himself to safeguard Bhera's cultural legacy.

During the Sikh rule in the 1700s, Bhera was home to enterprising, education-loving, and wealth-accumulating families such as the Sahni, Sethi, Kohli, Suri, Piracha, and Sheikh - some even claiming direct descent from Porus's Mohyal clan. Bhera retained its prominence during the reign of Maharaja Ranjit Singh, and it was during this period that a '*taksal*' (mint) was established in the town.

In the late 1700s or early 1800s, many families of the Sethi clan migrated from Bhera to Peshawar, where they converted to Islam while retaining their surname, "Sethi," a tradition that continues to this day.

The Hindu families of Bhera were known for their wealth and prosperity. It is said that they concealed their surplus gold and precious metals by stringing them into long wires, coating them with tar, and nailing them to the roofs of their *havelis*.

There are also stories of families burying their treasures before leaving Bhera at the time of Partition, hoping to return one day and reclaim them. Some Muslim families who were later allotted these homes occasionally discovered these hidden riches.

The last chief or Raja of Bhera was a '*Sethi Khukhrain*', Diwan Bahadur Jawahar Mal.

The Diwan family originally came from Peshawar and tradition ascribes the abolition of 'Jizya' *(tax levied on non-Muslim's in return for protection and the ability to practice their faith)* in Peshawar to his influence.

Bhera station, where trains don't stop anymore

Bhera was located at the terminus of the Northwestern Railway network and was known for its important changeover track. The foundation of Bhera Railway Station was laid in 1881 during the British Raj. During its operational period, a train ran between Bhera and Malakwal Junction, covering a distance of 28 kilometres. Initially, steam locomotives were used, later replaced by diesel engines.

In 2005, Pakistan Railways closed Bhera Station due to a lack of profitability. Once a site of grandeur - where a wealthy Hindu merchant famously rolled out a red carpet from the platform to his doorstep to welcome a British guest - the station now stands abandoned and eerie.

Neglect and vandalism led to the gradual dismantling of the station. The bricks, doors, and even the foundations of the station master's and staff residences were stolen. The main railway station building, including the passenger hall, canteen, booking office, parcel warehouse, station master's office, and the first-class passenger lodge, was stripped of its furniture, doors, fans, and electrical wiring.

The railway tracks themselves disappeared, and as the platform crumbled, local residents began using the abandoned railway buildings to shelter their livestock. A once-thriving hub of activity had turned into a haunting relic of the past.

A crumbling police station built in 1870 still stands as a mute witness to the ravages the town of Bhera has suffered.

About 10 miles from Bhera lies the village of Mong, known in Greek as *Nicaea* (Victory), where Alexander the Great is believed to have fought King Porus in 326 B.C. Porus, a *Vaid Mohiyal*, is said to have fiercely resisted Alexander's army. Some Mohiyal traditions claim that Alexander, rather than emerging victorious, suffered heavy losses in the battle. Alexander's beloved horse, Bucephalus, was killed in combat, allegedly by Porus's son, and is buried in the nearby town of Jalalpur, across the western side of the Jhelum River. This account is documented in the *'District Gazetteer of Jhelum – 1904'*, republished by *'Sang-e-Meel, Lahore'* in 2004.

In the 1940s, Bhera's population was composed of approximately 1% Sikhs, 22% Hindus, and the remaining majority Muslims. Among the Muslim population were families such as the Sethi, Sheikh, and Piracha, who were themselves converts and had cultural and historical ties to the Hindu community.

Unlike many other parts of the subcontinent, Bhera did not witness bloodshed during Partition in 1947.

The local Muslim merchant class, particularly the Sheikh families, provided protection to the town's Hindu residents before their departure to India, ensuring a peaceful transition

An important citizen of Bhera (born 25th December 1850), Bakshi Ram Dass Chhibber, was a classic and a majestic *Mohyal (Saraswat Brahmin)* patriarch. Popularly known as Munshi Ram Dass, he was a tutor of Urdu and Persian to the ruling British. Amongst his pupils were such formidable personalities as Lord and Lady Minto, Lord and Lady Hardinge, Lady Curzon, Lady Lansdowne and Field Marshal Roberts, the *Commander in Chief* of India. He used his influence to get the Mohyals listed as agriculturists. On his request, Russell Stracey wrote the History of the Mohyals in 1911, which till now is the most reliable account of the venerable community. Bakshi Ram Dass was a philanthropist who gave Rs. 30,000/= to D.A.V. College, Lahore and Rs. 20,000/= to the General Mohyal Sabha in pre-1947.

Govt. High School, Bhera, 1927

The School's Inaugural Plaque

Today, Bhera is nestled amidst the scenic landscapes of the Jhelum River, the *'Khewra Salt Mines,* and the renowned *Kinowa* mandarin and orange orchards of Sargodha district.

Approximately 500 years ago, this region was densely forested and teeming with wildlife, including deer, *nilgai*, and *urial*. It is believed that Emperor Jahangir once hunted here, reportedly killing as many as 500 deer.

Present-day Bhera is a shadow of its former self, vastly different from the thriving town it once was. Once a flourishing hub at the crossroads of history, near present-day Sargodha, it has gradually faded into obscurity. Its significance has diminished over time, leaving behind crumbling structures and forgotten streets.

On the horizon of time, Bhera drifts toward oblivion. As a local folk verse from Bhera poignantly says...

"Bhera phullan da Sehra

Phull gaey murjhaa

Bhera rakh Leya Khuda"

It is also said that the Urdu proverb *"Bhera Paar"* originated from Bhera

CHAPTER 2

- THE SETHI CLAN "KHUKHRAINS"

KHUKHRAIN – THE WARRIOR CLAN

"Khukhrain", traditionally a warrior community, are specific clans, the count of which is usually placed to be eight of the Khatri caste. It is said that Porus who fought the army of Alexander as Purushottama, the king of Kekaya, land of the Puru tribe, was also a Khukhrain.

In Sanskrit "Khukhrain" is spelt as Kushrayan, meaning Descendants of King Kush, Progeny of King Padam Anand. They are Suryavanshi and direct descendants of King Raam of Ayodhya and that is why Maharishi Valmiki named the holy book of Hindu's as "Anand Ramayan".

The area of origin of Khukhrains was the Sind Sagar Doab (Indus-Jhelum interfluve) and the Jech Doab (Jhelum-Chenab interfluve) region of Pakistan that comprised Khushab, Dhune Kheb, Pindi Gheb, Talagang, Chakwal, Pindi Dadan Khan, Peshawar, Nowshera and Lahore.

The name "Doab" literally translates to "land of two rivers" ("Do" two, "Ab" river; Punjabi). In former India, Sind Sagar Doab and Jech Doab were the main region where Khukhrains were in large numbers. The language spoken in the region was majorly Doabi.

The clan faced the brunt of invasions from various Asian tribes now converted to Islam, who came to Bhera and Salt Range from the northwest during the 12th - 16th centuries.

The Khukhrains were a powerful tribe who refused to submit to foreigners resisting them at every opportunity.

It is said that during the reign of Khukhrain king, Raja Khokhar Mal women were encouraged to excel in archery, fencing and other martial arts. The clash of the Khukhrain's with Mahmud of Ghazni took place in his third invasion at the Battle of Bhadravati (Bhera) in 1004 -1005 CE, when he was returning from Somnath after having plundered a huge booty from the famous Shiva temple of Somnath. This plunder of Mahmud had shaken the religious sentiments of the Hindus, and it was in this area that the Khukhrains attacked his army and relieved him of a large part of the booty.

Women took part in the skirmish and thwarted the attempt of the invaders. About 30 women lost their lives to 20 Mongols in the battle. Ghazni who retreated to launch another attack, was later defeated, captured and held in captivity. After his release, he regrouped and provoked the clan by slaughtering a cow outside the palace temple.

The clan came out in full force but were defeated. Ghazni then turned his attention to the women of the clan. The women shamed him by reminding him of his period in captivity when he was treated with humanity. The clan, nevertheless, continued to grow and prosper.

In 1008 – 1009 CE, Mahmud Ghazni again attacked Bhera and ransacked it leading to the Khukhrain King Biji Rai committing suicide ending his life with his own dagger, rather than surrender.

In 326 BC, Alexander the Great, whose forces were then fighting against the army of King Porus, at the left bank of river Jhelum near Southern Salt Range, wrote in a letter to his mother and said:

"I am involved in the land of leonine (lion-like) and brave people called Khukhrain', where every foot of the ground is like a wall of steel, confronting my soldiers. You have brought only one son into the world, but everyone in this land can be called an Alexander".

Khukhrains included Kohli, Sahini, Sabharwal, Suri, Sethi, Bhasin, Anand and Chadha clans which later expanded to include four new subclans which were Chandok (Chandhoke, Chandhok, Chandiok), Chhachi (Chachi, Chhachhi), a sub section of the Kohli clan, and Ghai.

Most of the Khukhrain's who moved to India following the partition in 1947 descended from Doab region of Pakistan that comprised of Khushab, Pindi Gheb, Talagang, Campbellpur, Chakwal, Pind Dadan Khan, Peshawar and Nowshera.

Various contemporary and historical places in Pakistan Punjab and Afghanistan corresponding to traditional areas associated with Khukhrain or Khokhar bear the name or variants of Khukhrain or Kokrana.

The Khukhrain clan was originally Hindu. Later the clan members embraced Sikhism and Islam. Khukhrains of all these faiths collectively form one kinship. The conversion started in 12th century and continued till 1947. In the western districts of the Punjab (Sargodha, Mianwali, Multan, Jhang, Chakwal, Rawalpindi and Faisalabad) the converted Khukhrain Khatri traders called themselves "Khoja". They are also called "Khoja Sheikh"

In Pakistan there continues to be many Muslim Khukhrains living especially in the Pakistani Punjab. Some scholars believe that a number of Khukhrains were converted to Islam by the Sufi Baba Farid. Many Muslim Khukhrains (including Sethis) still use their pre-Islamic Hindu gotras.

The Khukhrain community is known for its vibrant social life, characterized by elaborate weddings, communal gatherings, and cultural events. Weddings are grand affairs, often lasting several days and featuring traditional music, dance forms like *'Bhangra'*, rituals and culinary delights such as *'Makke di Roti'*, *'Sarson da Saag'*, *'Chole Bhature'* and *'Lassi.'* These celebrations not only highlight their zest for life but also serve as a means of social bonding and reinforce the community's shared heritage and values.

The global diaspora of the Khukhrains has fostered a sense of cosmopolitanism while retaining strong ties to their cultural roots. Organizations and associations have been formed to promote community welfare, preserve cultural traditions, and support educational initiatives. These efforts ensure that the younger generation remains connected to their heritage and continue the legacy of their ancestors.

Education remains a cornerstone of the Khukhrain ethos. The community places a high value on academic achievement, and many Khukhrains occupy prominent positions in various professional fields. This emphasis on education and professional excellence has enabled the community to adapt to changing socio-economic landscapes while maintaining their distinct identity.

The Khukhrains are a testament to the enduring strength and adaptability of a community deeply rooted in history and tradition. Their journey from ancient Punjab to the present day is marked by resilience, enterprise, and a commitment to cultural preservation.

As the Khukhrains navigate the complexities of the modern world, they continue to draw inspiration from their rich heritage, contributing to the socio-economic and cultural fabric of the societies they inhabit. Through their achievements and traditions, the Khukhrains exemplify the dynamic interplay between historical legacy and contemporary relevance.

Today, Khukhrain Hindus or Sikhs are, by and large an urbanised highly educated and economically well-off community dispersed across various regions of India, with concentrations in Punjab, Haryana, Delhi and Uttar Pradesh. Khukhrains in India and Pakistan have excelled in almost all spheres including business, politics, arts, military and in various fields of science as well as in judiciary and law.

Among all Punjabi communities, the Khukhrains are the most respected and are counted as the topmost.

It is interesting to note some facts about the eight clans of Khukhrains and how they derived their names –

1. **ANAND** – Named after a common ancestor "Ananda", which in Sanskrit means "Joy" or "Happiness", "Feel of Heaven".

2. **BHASIN** – "Bhasin" derived from the Sanskrit word *'Bhuseen' means 'Power of Speech'. 'Bhu' (tongue / speech) 'Seen' (power)*. In some places it has been used for *"Sun"*. They were mostly concentrated in the district of Rawalpindi. According to the 1881 census of India conducted by British there were 1208 families in the Rawalpindi District.

3. **CHADHA** – Derived from the name of *'Chamunda'*, who was the slayer of evil. According to a local account, the ancestors of Chadhas fought with Babur in a war. However, all of them died except for one man who hid behind an *Aak (Rubber)* bush. This person continued the progeny of the Chadha clan. To pay tribute to the Aak bush which saved the Chadha clan from extinction, the Chadhas visit Eminabad in Gujranwala district to perform prayers and worship the Aak tree as a former tradition.

4. **KOHLI** – The word is *'Kul Hari'*, based on the name of one of the goddesses of North India *(Kul Devi)* and *'Lord Vishnu' (Hari),* the one who preserves *"The Preserver"*. The word *'Hari'* came into existence in the holy book *'Mahabharat'* in which it means *'One who takes away'*. It is widely believed among Khukhrain's that their continuance and survival till the present day is owing to their preserving by the Kohli clan. Another version believes that the Prakrit word *"Koh"* means a "mountain" and they lived in the hilly tracks of Hazara and Rawalpindi.

5. **SABHARWAL** – Derived from the Sanskrit word *"Shubh Var"*, which means *"the lucky one"*. It is mentioned in *Bhai Gurdas's Vaar 11*. Bhai Tirtha was the leader among all Sikhs of Sabharwal sub-caste. The surname originated among the Sikh Khatris of the Punjab region.

6. **SAHNI** (Sawhney) – The word *"Sahni"* is derived from *"Senani"*, meaning *"General of an Army"* or *'Chief Commander'*. They were the inhabitants of Bhera town on the eastern bank of Jhelum River prior to the partition. Sahni families were also the governors of Wazirabad tehsil.

7. **SETHI** – This surname is derived from the Sanskrit word *"Srestha"* meaning *"Pure"*, *"Superior"*, *"The Best among all"*. It also denotes the head of a mercantile or other guild.

8. **SURI** – The word Suri is used in both Vedic and classical Sanskrit for *"Sun"* or *"Brightness of Sun"*. Originating from Suri Dynasty's ruler Sher Shah Suri they represent themselves as his descendants. *'Suri*, also translates to *"Shaurya"* or *"Shoor Vir (the most courageous)"*

As our surnames and family names represent our ancestors, 'Gotra' represents the name of the 'Rishi' who was the father of our ancestors.

Regarding the *'Gotra'*, Khukhrains original Gotra is *'Kashyap'*. Among the eight clans - Anands, Kohlis and Bhasins maintained their original *'Kashyap Gotra'* while the other five clans due to change of *'Purohit's (Guru)'* of their times started to accept different gotra's of their own.

In Hindu rituals *(Prarthana, Havan etc.)* the three clans of Anands, Kohlis and Bhasins say, *"Kashyap Gotra Utpanah* (birth) whereas the other five clans, Chadhas, Sabharwals, Sahnis, Sethis and Suris say *'Dhaaran' (accepted)*, because their guru's or purohits have given them their present gotra and their ancestors *"adopted"* them.

THE KHUKHRAIN VANSHAVALI

KHUKRAIN CLAN	VANSH	GOTRA	PUROHIT	KUL DEVTA	STAMBH	NAME OF KING	CAPITAL	JURISDICTION OF KINGDOM
ANAND	Surya	Kashyap	Beejra	Durga Ma	Chandrama	Maharaja Dhananand	Takshila (Bhera)	Takshila to Bhera Bhera to Sargodha
BHASIN	Surya	Kashyap	Beejra	Durga Ma	Chandrama	Raja Bhuseen	Salvan Nagar (Sialkot)	Sialkot to Jammu Sialkot to Gujrat
CHADHA	Surya	Veervansh	Lau	Baba Sodal	Agni	Raja Chamunda	Lanpur (Lahore)	Lahore to Gujrat
KOHLI	Surya	Kashyap	Dant	Bhadrakali	Chandrama	Raja Kualhari	Jullandhar (Jallandhar)	Jallandhar to Amritsar Jallandhar to Hoshiarpur
SABHARWAL	Surya	Hanslas	Madan Svambh	Baba Medar	Chandrama	Raja Subharvar	Purushwar (Peshawar)	Peshawar to Hindu Kush Peshawar to Rawalpindi
SAHNI	Surya	Veervansh	Vasudev	Bhadrakali	Surya	Raja Sheshshaini	Roopwal (Rawalpindi)	Rawalpindi to Gujur Khan Rawalpindi to Kala Bagh to Pindi
SETHI	Surya	Pulastya	Sudhan	Vaishno Devi	Chandrama	Raja Surathraj	Jhelum (Virat Nagar) Ktakshruj (Katasraj)	Virat Nagar to Kotsarang (Swargang) via Talangang Kotsarang to Peshawar via Pindi Gheb
SURI	Surya	Bhargav	Panda	Sheshnag	Chandrama	Raja Shoorsen	Kushpur (Kasur)	Kasur to Lahore Kasur to Amritsar

CHAPTER 3

- THE "SETHI" TITLE – MEANING and HISTORY

THE SETHIS – A BRIEF HISTORY

The name "Sethi" is derived from the Sanskrit word "*Sreshta*," meaning '*Pure*', '*Superior*', or the '*Best among all*'. It also denotes the head of a mercantile or other guild. The Sethis have also been called "*Pulseti*," based on their gotra '*Pulastya*.'

The Sethi clan belongs to the warrior community known as the "*Khukhrains*," a derivative of "*Khokhar*" or "*Khukhr*i," a lethal dagger they historically carried. The present day Sethis are descendants of *Raja Khokhar Mal* who ruled a part of West Punjab with his seat at Bhera. He was instrumental in forging unity of all other sections and laid the foundation of a single powerful kingdom, which came to be known as '*Khukhrain Clan*'. Originally Sethi's were wealthy traders from Peshawar, part of the clan migrated to Bhera in the early 18th century.

The Sethis were among the bravest Khukhrain clans. So formidable were they that during Mahmud Ghazni's third invasion of India (1004-1005 CE), he instructed his generals to avoid antagonizing them after the battle of Bhera.

The Sethis are one of the eight original Khukhrain clans - Anand, Kohli, Suri, Bhasin, Sahni, Chadha, Sethi, and Sabharwal - which later expanded to include Chandok (Chandhoke, Chandhok, Chandiok), Chhachi (a sub-section of the Kohli clan), and Ghai. These clans share a common ancestry and have traditionally maintained close ties through social networks and intermarriage.

Prominence During Medieval and Mughal Eras

During the medieval and Mughal periods, the Sethi's and other Khukhrain's rose to prominence due to their strategic acumen and business skills. They served as administrators and military leaders under various rulers and became influential merchants, significantly contributing to the region's economic prosperity. This period saw the Khukhrains, including the Sethis, establishing themselves as key figures in the socio-economic and political landscape of Punjab.

Migration and Impact of Partition (1947) - The migration of the Sethi clan, a sub-caste of the Khatri community, is a significant chapter in South Asian history. Particularly impacted by the partition of India in 1947, the Sethi families' migration from Bhera, now in Pakistan, to various parts of India and beyond is a tale of resilience, adaptation, and continuity of cultural heritage.

Bhera, a historically significant town in the Sargodha district of Punjab (Pakistan), was historically a significant town. It was a hub of trade, culture, and learning, with a diverse population that included various communities such as the Khukhrains. The Sethis played a vital role in its economy and social fabric.

The partition of India in 1947 was a cataclysmic event that led to one of the largest mass migrations in human history. The partition created the separate states of India and Pakistan, leading to widespread communal violence, displacement, and loss of life. The Punjab region, where Bhera is located, was particularly affected due to its mixed Hindu, Sikh, and Muslim population.

However, partition triggered one of the largest mass migrations in human history, driven by:

1. **Communal Violence and Safety Concerns** – The widespread violence following partition forced Hindu and Sikh families, including the Sethis, to flee their ancestral homes.

2. **Religious Division** – The new geopolitical landscape made it difficult for non-Muslims to remain in Pakistan without facing discrimination or violence.

3. **Economic Disruption** – Partition disrupted businesses and livelihoods, compelling many families to seek stability in India.

The journey to India was perilous, involving travel by foot, train, or makeshift transportation, with many families facing extreme hardship. Upon arrival, they had to rebuild their lives from scratch. Despite initial struggles, the Sethi's leveraged their resilience and entrepreneurial spirit to re-establish themselves successfully.

Contributions and Achievements

Over the years, the Sethi clan has made significant contributions across various fields:

1. **Business and Commerce** – Continuing their legacy of entrepreneurship, the Sethis established successful enterprises, contributing to economic growth.

2. **Education and Professional Excellence** – Many Sethis pursued higher education and excelled in medicine, engineering, law, academia, and other professional fields. Their success in these fields further cemented their reputation as a robust and capable community.

3. **Cultural Preservation** – The community actively preserves its heritage through organizations, festivals, and linguistic traditions ensuring that the younger generations remain connected to their roots.

4. **Philanthropy and Social Service** – Many have contributed to educational and healthcare initiatives, supporting charitable causes thus giving back to society and supporting those in need.

Global Diaspora - Following partition, the Sethi migration did not stop at India. Over the subsequent years many moved further to the United States, Canada, the United Kingdom, and Australia, forming a global network of Sethi families. Despite settling in diverse regions, they maintain strong community ties and continue contributing to a diverse array of professional and cultural spheres.

Cultural and Social Life - The Sethis are an Indo-Scythian community and like other Khukhrains, have historically followed Hinduism, with a significant number adopting Sikhism in the 18th and 19th centuries. Many Hindu Khukhrains continue to practice both Sikh and Arya Samaj traditions. Their religious observances include major festivals such as Diwali, Holi, Vaisakhi, and Gurupurab, reflecting their blended heritage.

The Sethi mother tongue is Punjabi, though dialects vary between those in Pakistan and East Punjab. The community is known for its vibrant social life, with grand weddings, communal gatherings, and cultural events like "Mundan" etc. strengthening social bonds.

Weddings are particularly grand, often spanning several days and featuring traditional music, dance forms like *'Bhangra'*, rituals and culinary delights such as *'Makke di Roti'*, *'Sarson da Saag'*, *'Chole Bhature'* and *'Lassi.'* These celebrations not only serve as a means of social bonding but also reinforce the community's shared heritage and values.

Legacy and Modern Influence - The Khukhrain community, including the Sethis, places a high value on education and entrepreneurship. Historically, the community has produced numerous scholars, writers, and business leaders. The emphasis on academic achievement and professional excellence continues to this day, with many Sethis occupying prominent positions in various professional fields. This focus on education has enabled the community to adapt to changing socio-economic landscapes while maintaining their distinct identity.

The global diaspora of the Sethi clan has fostered a sense of cosmopolitanism while retaining strong ties to their cultural roots. Organizations and associations have been formed to promote community welfare, preserve cultural traditions, and support educational initiatives. These efforts ensure that the younger generation remains connected to their heritage and continues the legacy of their ancestors.

The Sethi clan, as part of the Khukhrain sub-caste of the Khatri community, has a rich and enduring heritage. From their ancient roots in Punjab to their prominence during the Mughal era and their resilience in the face of post-partition challenges, the Sethis exemplify a dynamic interplay between historical legacy and contemporary relevance. Their commitment to education, cultural preservation, and social service continues to define the community, ensuring that the Sethi name remains influential and respected in the modern world.

The Sethis have always been a very powerful and wealthy group of the Punjabi community especially those living in large cities, either in Pakistan or now in India. Through their achievements and traditions, the Sethis today remain a dynamic and influential community, contributing significantly to the socio-economic and cultural fabric of their adopted societies.

MOHALLA SETHIAN and SETHI HAVELIS IN PESHAWAR

The Sethi families of Peshawar trace their origin to Bhera, from where they migrated during the Sikh rule in Punjab. Initially settling in Chamkani, a small village across the River Bara, they later moved to Peshawar City. Renowned as successful businessmen and traders, the Sethis amassed great wealth through trade with India, Afghanistan, Russia, and Central Asia. Beyond their commercial success, they were also generous philanthropists, funding public welfare projects such as the construction of mosques and bridges. At the heart of Peshawar's historic old city lies *'Mohalla Sethian,'* home to the iconic Sethi Havelis, built between 1823 and the 1920s. These havelis showcase exquisite 18th and 19th century architecture, reflecting a blend of Bukhara, Kashmiri, Golconda, and Iranian artistic influences.

 The most distinguished among them is the 'Sethi Haveli,' constructed in 1884 by the affluent Karim Baksh Sethi. In 2006, the Directorate of Archaeology and Museums, Khyber Pakhtunkhwa, acquired the haveli to preserve its historical significance. Located in Mohalla Sethian, near Bazar Kalan on Tehsil Ghanta Ghar Road, Peshawar City, it spans an area of 33 marlas.

This three storied haveli comprises a '*Tehkhana*' (basement), '*Balakhana*' (upper floor), and a grand triple-arched entrance into a courtyard. Designed in a traditional oriental style, it features intricately carved wooden doors and windows, beautifully painted ceilings, and fresco adorned walls. Its architectural brilliance also includes an advanced system for natural light and ventilation. Restored by the Archaeology Department, the haveli now stands as a prominent tourist attraction, offering visitors a glimpse into Peshawar's rich cultural and architectural heritage.

THE VANSHAVALI OF THE SETHIS

VANSH	SURYA
GOTRA	PULASTYA
PUROHIT	SUDHAN
KUL DEVTA	VAISHNO DEVI
STAMBH	CHANDRAMA
NAME OF KING	RAJA SURATHRAJ
CAPITAL	JHELUM (VIRAT NAGAR)
	KTAKSHRUJ (KATASRAJ)
JURISDICTION OF KINGDOM	VURATNAGAR TO KOTSARANG (SWARGANG) VIA TALANGAN
	KOTSARANG TO PESHAWAR VIA PINDI GHEB

CHAPTER 4

- OUR ANCESTORS

OUR ANCESTORS

The Sethi Family tree which I was able to compile with the help of the weathered note penned by my father and help from my relatives goes eight generations above me and my immediate cousins and four generations after us. So, we have some details of the thirteen generations of The Sethi family tree.

The earliest known details available are of my Great - Great – Grandfather, **Dani Ditta Lal Sethi** who was born around 1800.

Dani Ditta Lal Sethi had two brothers, **Gulab Chand Sethi** and **Shiv Dayal Sethi**. They were preceded by **Ram Kishan Sethi – Sukh Anand Sethi – Harjas Rai Sethi – Kulwant Rai Sethi**.

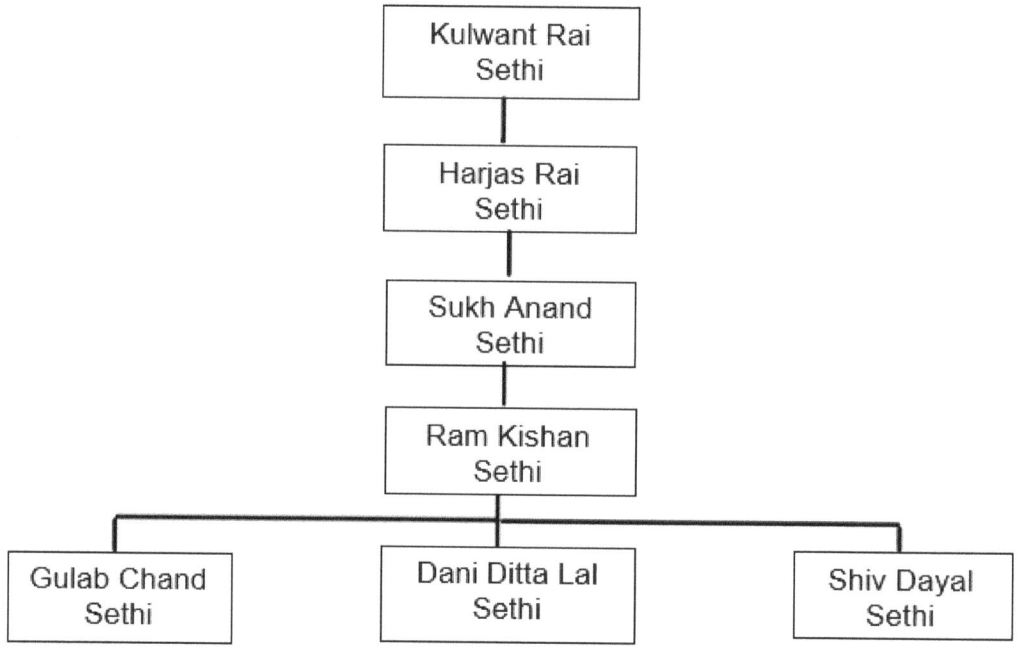

As per records available, **Dani Ditta Lal Sethi** was born in 1800, so it can be safely assumed that his brothers, **Gulab Chand Sethi** and **Shiv Dayal Sethi** were born between 1802-1804. As such their Father **Ram Kishan Sethi** may have been born around 1770 and his father **Sukh Anand Sethi** around 1740, **Harjas Rai Sethi** around 1730 and **Kulwant Rai Sethi** around 1700.

Dani Ditta Lal Sethi was born in Bhera in the district of Shahpur, Sargodha. He was a landlord and later migrated from Bhera to Rawalpindi along with one of his brothers around the year 1850. Before migrating from Bhera to Rawalpindi, he carried with him some coins and about 50 Kaoris (a kind of small seashell variety) prevalent around those times for purchase of daily necessities of life. They purchased some landed property in Rawalpindi and later returned to Bhera.

During that time my Great Grandfather, **Lala Narsingh Das Sethi** was just a child and studying with a '*Pandha*' (a village teacher). In 1850 when Lala Narsingh Das Sethi was around 25 years old, Dani Ditta Lal Sethi, along with his brother Gulab Chand Sethi and their respective families left Bhera and migrated to Rawalpindi where he had already purchased some landed property.

The third brother Shiv Dayal Sethi stayed back at Bhera to look after the land and family houses. However, whenever there was any family function Dani Ditta Lal Sethi along with the whole family used to go to Bhera for the celebrations and the complete joint family used to get together.

The war was a boon for Dani Ditta Lal Sethi, who helped in pushing the enemy back and was rewarded with a good booty. Unfortunately, his other two brothers Gulab Chand Sethi and Shiv Dayal Sethi felt very jealous and parted from the main family and started living separately.

Dani Ditta Lal Sethi died at the age of 90 years in the year 1890 when his son Narsingh Das Sethi was around 65 years old.

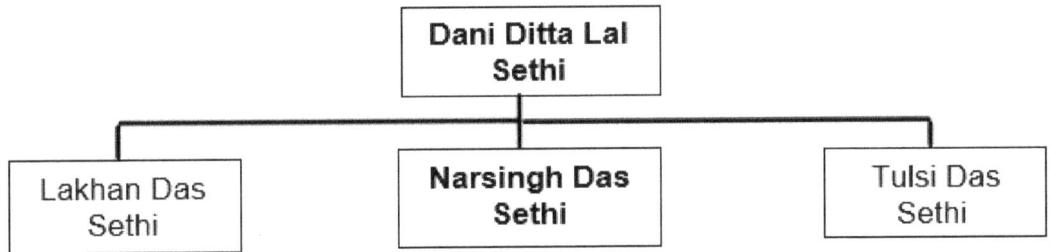

Lakhan Das Sethi, Narsingh Das Sethi's brother had two sons Pindi Das Sethi and Manohar Lal Sethi.

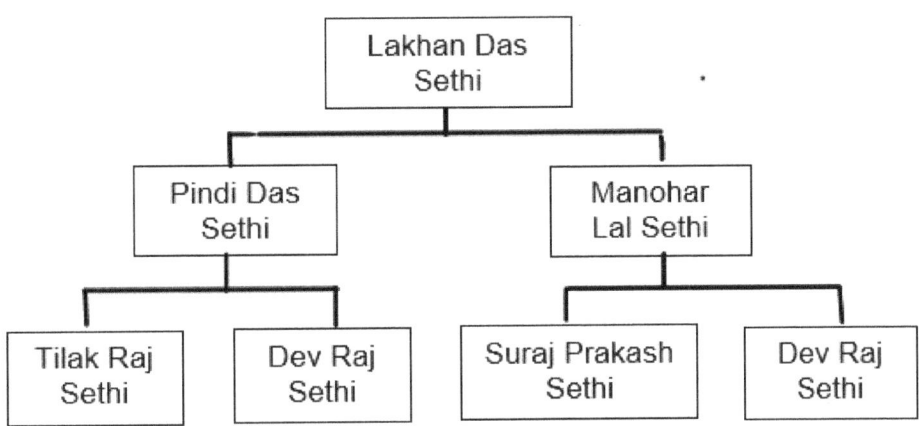

Pindi Das Sethi had two sons, Tilak Raj Sethi and Dev Raj Sethi.

Manohar Lal Sethi also had two sons, Suraj Prakash Sethi and Devraj Sethi. Unfortunately, presently there are no details about them nor records of their further lineage.

The other brother of Narsingh Das Sethi, Tulsi Das Sethi had three sons, Madhusudan Lal Sethi, Hari Ram Sethi and Harbans Lal Sethi. No details or lineage records of Madhusudan Lal Sethi and Hari Ram Sethi are presently available.

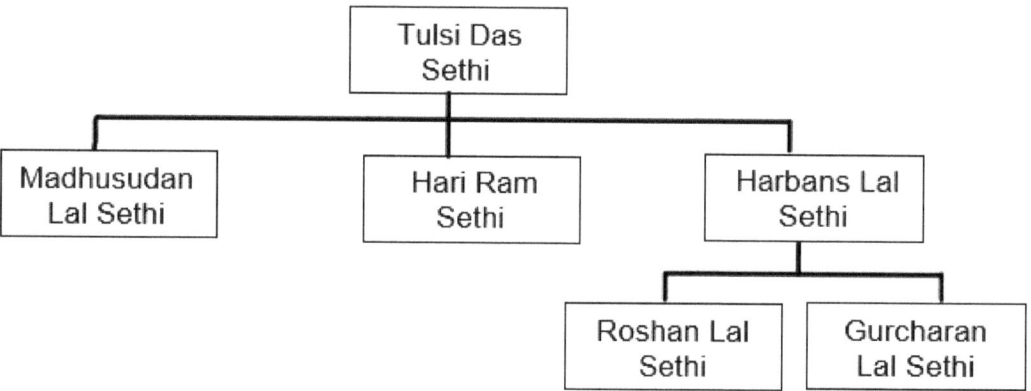

However, their other brother Harbans Lal Sethi had two sons, namely, Roshan Lal Sethi and Gurcharan Lal Sethi.

Despite my best efforts, I was unable to get any details pertaining to the personal and family details nor the whereabouts of the families of Narsingh Das Sethi's brothers, except the family tree shown above.

I do recall that when I was about 8 years old my father mentioned that one branch of his grandfather's family (Narsingh Das Sethi's brother) or Great Grandfather's family (Dani Ditta Lal Sethi's brother) had migrated to Peshawar, and some stayed back in Rawalpindi/Lahore/Bhera.

I made every effort to connect with Sethi families, both Hindu and those who had converted to Islam, living in Peshawar, Rawalpindi, and Lahore. However, none had records beyond their immediate family, making it impossible to trace any ancestral links to our family tree.

Perhaps one day, one of us may come across a Sethi descendant who shares a connection with our lineage.

CHAPTER 5

- THE FAMILY IN PRESENT TIMES

MY FAMILY – FIRST SIX GENERATIONS

My Great Grand Father **Narsingh Das Sethi** son of Dani Ditta Lal Sethi, grandson of Ram Kishan Sethi, great - great grandson of Sukhanand Sethi, great - great - great grandson of Harjas Rai Sethi and great - great - great - great grandson of Kulwant Rai Sethi was the 6th generation "Sethi "as per the details available.

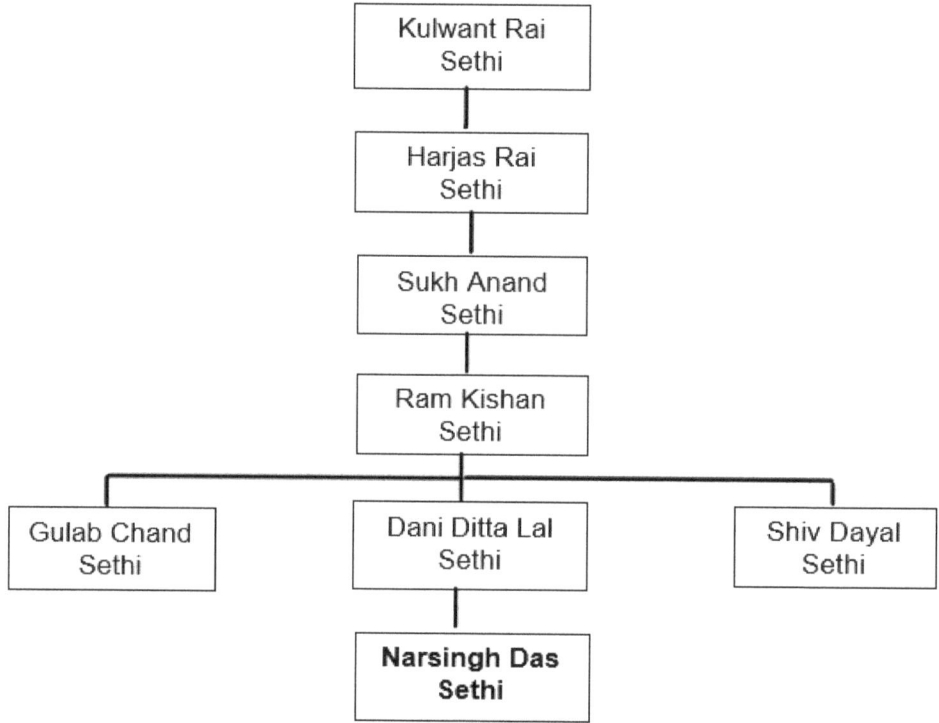

Narsingh Das Sethi, was born in Bhera, Sargodha district, now in Pakistan. He was a very wise man.

After the Great Mutiny and the first Independence in 1857 there was great unrest and panic in U.P. and Punjab. During that period **Narsingh Das Sethi** took up some dealings in Gold, Silver, Lead, used cartridges and allied materials for which there was a great demand by the British government as they wanted to quell the internal unrest in the country. Also, during that period the Afghan war was happening on the "frontier side". These circumstances proved to be a boon, and his business flourished.

Narsingh Das Sethi had three children, namely a daughter Ishara Devi, **Lala Ganesh Das Sethi** (my grandfather) and Bodh Raj Sethi. Ishara Devi was the eldest and was married to Diwan Das Raj Sawhney a very famous family of landlords in Bhera. Diwan Das Raj Sawhney, her husband was a very well-known Bar-at-Law.

Bodh Raj Sethi was married to Jivan Deyi Sethi who was from the Chandok family.

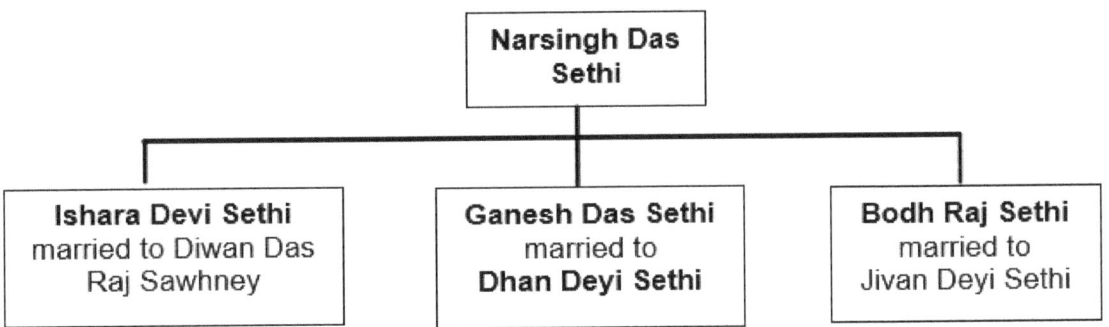

SEVENTH GENERATION

Ganesh Das Sethi got married to **Dhan Deyi Sethi**, the only daughter of Doctor Bhagat Ram Sawhney who during those days was the first person from Punjab to go abroad to study medicine and returned as the first Indian Civil Surgeon. He was awarded the title of "Rai Bahadur" by the British Government.

An interesting incident related to the wedding was much talked about. It is said that all cousins and other relatives of Dr. Bhagat Ram Sawhney (Ganesh Das Sethi father-in-law) refused to take "Shagun" (*distribution of sweets to relatives during a wedding*) saying that Dr. Sawhney has come from "Sat Samundar Paar" (abroad) and was wearing an "*English Dress*" (Suit) which made the marriage unreligious and against the Hindu law.

However, Narsingh Das Sethi (father of the groom) was least bothered about the boycott of the wedding and celebrated it in a grand manner with his friends. According to a document written by my uncle (Tayaji), Chaman Lal Sethi the wedding was a grand show and was said to be the best marriage ever performed in Bhera.

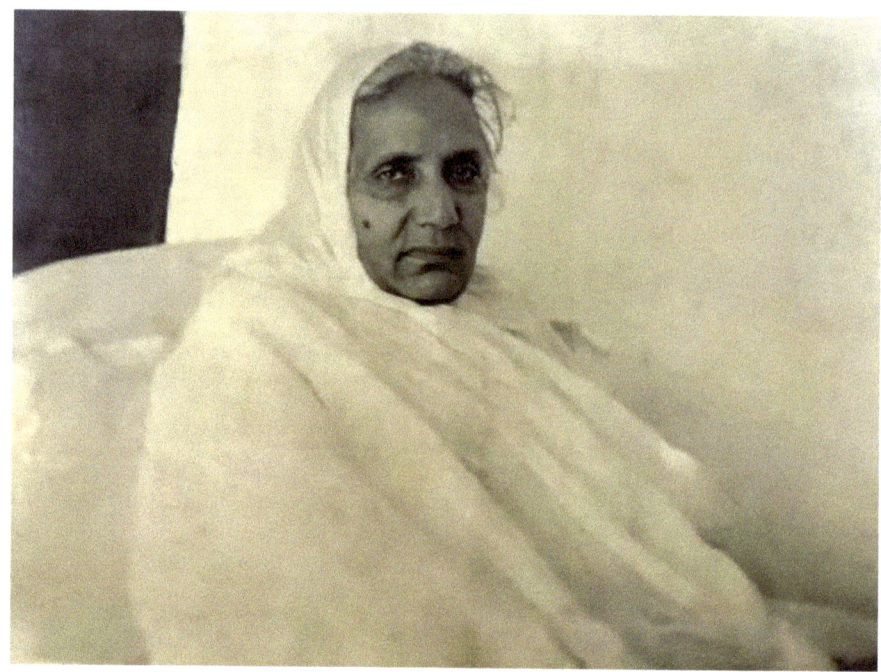

Dhan Deyi Sethi (Sawhney)

Dhan Deyi Sethi was the eldest of her three brothers, Mr. Dhan Raj Sawhney, Superintendent. Engineer, Dr. Mulk Raj Sawhney, ENT Specialist in Lahore and Mr. Dev Raj Sawhney, a very renowned Barrister.

Dr. Bhagat Ram Sawhney (Dhan Deyi Sethi father) was looked upon with hatred when he attended the civil hospital as he used to be the only Indian wearing an English hat. This infuriated him so much that he resigned from his I.M.S. Service and renounced his title of "Rai Bahadur". He then joined Maharaja Partap Singh of Jammu and Kashmir as his family doctor.

His two brothers, Lala Hans Raj Sawhney and Lala Gurdas Ram Sawhney, both barristers in Rawalpindi, were close friends of Lala Lajpat Rai and the great revolutionary Lala Hardayal. Both the brothers were arrested in 1907 for suspected burning of the Rawalpindi District Court and were exiled. They later moved to England and upon their return from England both brothers decided to convert to Christianity along with their families. But a chance meeting with Swami Dayanand Saraswati and his timely intervention and advice convinced them to change their decision. They then founded and laid the foundation stone for Arya Samaj and Arya Samaj School in Rawalpindi.

After Narsingh Das Sethi's death at the age of 75 in the year 1900, Ganesh Das Sethi and his brother Bodh Raj Sethi jointly ran the jewellery business "*Pindi Jewellers*" which their father had set up.

Ganesh Das Sethi was a rich man. Apart from the Gold and Jewellery business he also held a licence to supply raw material to the government for the manufacture of ammunition to be used in the Afghan war. He held many properties in Rawalpindi city and in the cantonment as also some houses and land in Bhera.

His brother Bodh Raj Sethi did not have any children. Soon after Narsingh Das Sethi's death one of the cousins of Bodh Raj Sethi instigated him to separate from the business and the family.

Ganesh Das Sethi, sensing some trouble and mischief called Bodh Raj Sethi and handed over the charge of the business to him. He told him that from then on, he should run the business and take care of the whole family and their needs, while Ganesh Das would maintain the accounts and look after the shops they owned in the city and cantonment, that were rented out. This, gesture, supposedly paved the way for the smooth running of the business and kept the family together. The family business was shut down after the passing of Lala Ganesh Das Sethi who died in 1929.

A quote from the memoirs of my Tayaji, Chamanlal Sethi – *"We never asked anything for our necessities from our father. Our uncle (Bodh Raj Sethi) was very gentle and loved us immensely and used to provide us with all that we needed and had a good control in the family"*

Lala Ganesh Das Sethi and his wife had 9 children, 4 sons and 5 daughters. It was indeed a large family. On a lighter note – Dhan Deyi Sethi really gave a Dhan *(Treasure)* of 9 children.

EIGHTH GENERATION

Amolak Ram Sethi (Ganesh Das Sethi eldest) was born on 13th August 1894 was the eldest and Narendra Nath Sethi (my father) born on 3rd November 1919 was the youngest. Wow! A gap of 25 years.

The eldest brother, Amolak Ram Sethi was 6 years older to Dina Nath Sethi, 10 years older to Chaman Lal Sethi and 25 years older to the youngest brother Narendra Nath Sethi.

All the brothers and sisters were terrified of the eldest brother Amolak Ram but at the same time had great respect for him as he held the family together and was very keen that all brothers get a good education.

He often used to ask them about their studies and if they were facing any difficulties. In fact, if any brother got a bad result in the exams he would not be spared and had to face his anger and often get beaten up.

The maximum brunt was borne by the two brothers Dina Nath and Chaman Lal and nobody in the family had the guts to interfere. Narendra Nath being 25 years younger was treated more as a son.

After their father's death in 1929 till the partition of the country the brothers remained united by all the decisions taken by the eldest brother Amolak Ram.

He ensured that his brothers got the best education and arranged for their conveniences, encouraging them to fulfil their dreams and ambitions.

The regard and respect the brothers had for their eldest brother, who was more of a father figure, is evident in this excerpt from Chaman Lal Sethi memoir:

ASSOCIATION & UNITY AMONG BROTHERS

My elder brother was 6 years elder to Dina Nath and 10 years elder to me, and 12 years elder to my younger brother Narinder. We all brothers and sisters were very afraid of our elder brother. Actually he was a terror for us all, besides his good hold in the family affairs. He was keen, that we brothers should get good education, so off and on, he would come and enquire about our studies and difficulties if any. He would not spare and beat us angerly, if any of us showed poor result in the exams. My brother Dina Nath and myself had a good brunt of it, as nobody in the family would interfere in his say or doing. After leaving my Victoria Diamond Jubilee Technical Institute Lahore half way he got very angry and upset, when my principal phoned him of my decision. The next morning I took the train for Rawalpindi without telling any brother. After our father's death in 1929 till partition of the country we all brothers, remained united by all the decisions, taken by our elder brother. He was just like a father to us, and loved us most. Even after the partition, we all had one voice. As both my elder brothers were out of Rawalpindi, I had to manage everything for the family, and look after the property and repairs and collection of rents.

GANESH DAS SETHI CHILDREN AND THEIR FAMILIES

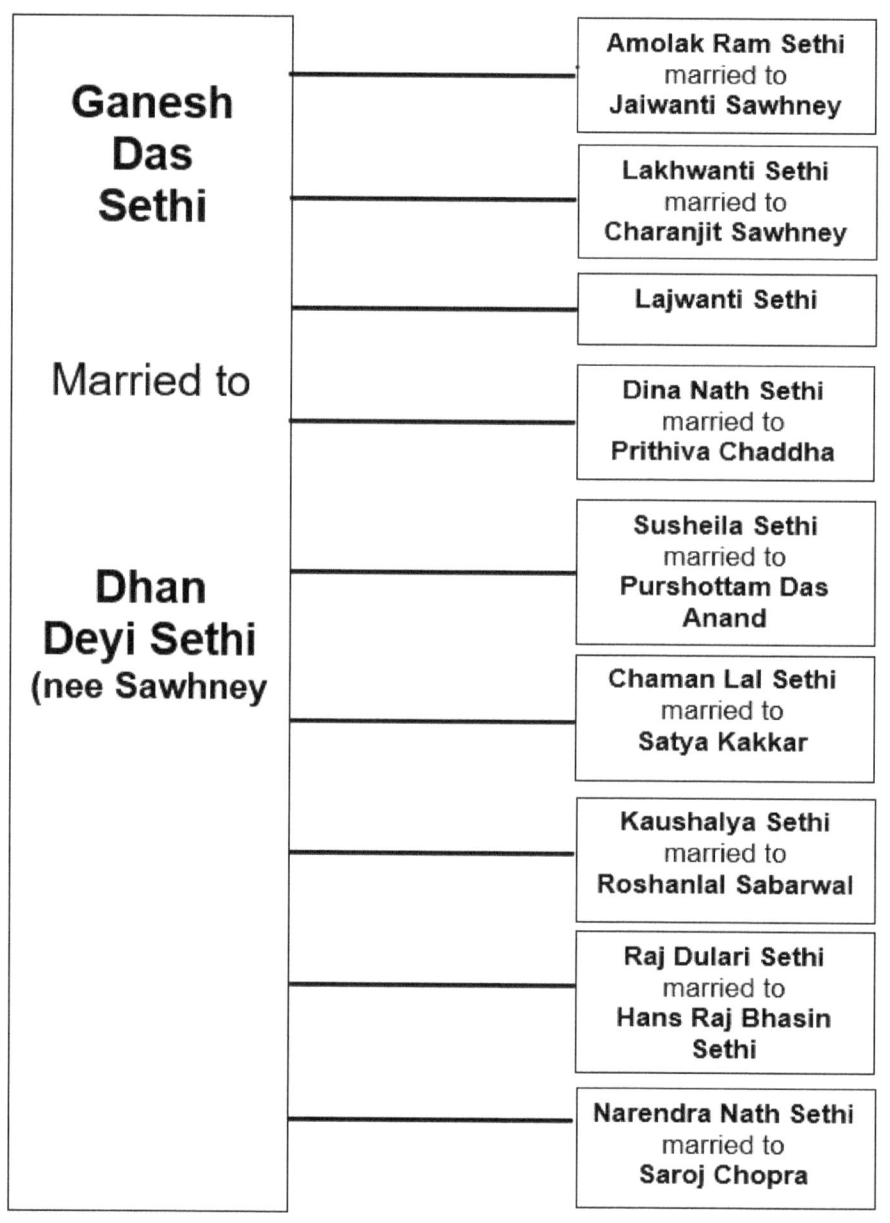

Kulwant Rai Sethi – Harjas Rai Sethi – Sukhanand Sethi – Ram Krishan Sethi – Dani Ditta Lal Sethi – Narsingh Das Sethi – Ganesh Das Sethi – Amolak Ram Sethi

AMOLAK RAM SETHI

Amolak Ram Sethi was born in Rawalpindi on 13th August 1894 and got married to Jaiwanti Sawhney on 25th September 1917 at Bhera. Jaiwanti, born in 1903 was the daughter of Lala Dhanpat Rai Sawhney, a Zamindar of Bhera. Amolak Ram was called "Papaji" by all, including his brothers and nephews and nieces and Jaiwanti was called as "Mataji.

Before Partition Papaji was in Rawalpindi where his father had a thriving jewellery business. Since Papaji was not interested in his father's jewellery business, he went to Lahore to get a job where he joined Reliable Water Supply as their general manager and with his efforts the firm developed into a successful and a profitable company and opened a branch in Lucknow. In Lahore he built a large house where all his children were born and educated before the partition of the country,

In June/July 1947 there were riots in Lahore and Papaji, while driving, narrowly escaped a bullet fired at him. He then decided to shift to Lucknow where his company had already established a branch office and remain there till the situation calmed down. However, the partition came as a blow, and they could never go back. Amolak Ram Sethi left for his heavenly abode on 5th April 1967 and Jaiwanti died on 8th October 1975.

Amolak Ram and Jaiwanti had 6 children, the eldest, Tilak Raj, born on 8th March 1924, Pushpa, born on 23rd November 1925, Kuldip, born on 4th May 1929, Yag, born on 26th July 1933, Rajinder (Raj), born on 12th September 1935 and the youngest, Kanchan, born on 31st August 1938.

Kulwant Rai Sethi – Harjas Rai Sethi – Sukhanand Sethi – Ram Krishan Sethi – Dani Ditta Lal Sethi – Narsingh Das Sethi – Ganesh Das Sethi – Lajwanti Sethi

LAJWANTI SETHI

Lajwanti died at a very young age and was never married.

Kulwant Rai Sethi – Harjas Rai Sethi – Sukhanand Sethi – Ram Krishan Sethi – Dani Ditta Lal Sethi – Narsingh Das Sethi – Ganesh Das Sethi – Lakhwanti Sethi

LAKHWANTI SETHI

Lakhwanti was married to Diwan Charanjit Sawhney, who was a businessman and had a big Electrical equipment showroom and a contract business in Lahore. For several years, he lived in Japan too.

The famous actor Balraj Sawhney and writer Bhisham Sawhney were his first cousins. Lakhwanti and Charanjit Sawhney had 9 children, Ravinder, Basant, Rajinder (Rajan), Kanta, Yog, Ashok, Krishan, Surinder and Vijay.

Kulwant Rai Sethi – Harjas Rai Sethi – Sukhanand Sethi – Ram Krishan Sethi – Dani Ditta Lal Sethi – Narsingh Das Sethi – Ganesh Das Sethi – Dina Nath Sethi

DINA NATH SETHI

Dina Nath Sethi was born in Rawalpindi. Having studied engineering, he joined the Sugar Industry and headed sugar mills in Rampur, Bareilly and Siwan. Dina Nath Sethi married Preetiva who was well educated and had studied in a convent school. She was also one of the first Indian women to study up to graduation.

They had two sons Lalit (Sonny) and Parimal Kumar (Pimmi) and two daughters Janak, born on 24th October 1930 and Meera (Cuckoo) born on 8th August 1940. After the death of Dina Nath Sethi the family, Janak Parimal and Meera along with their mother Preetiva shifted to Lucknow.

Preetiva died in a very tragic incident. A robber entered their house one night and Preetiva woke up and was about to scream for help on spotting the robber when the robber killed her.

Kulwant Rai Sethi – Harjas Rai Sethi – Sukhanand Sethi – Ram Krishan Sethi – Dani Ditta Lal Sethi – Narsingh Das Sethi – Ganesh Das Sethi – Susheila Sethi

SUSHEILA SETHI

Susheila (Sheila) was born in February 1906 in Bhera. She studied in Rawalpindi and got married around the year 1929 in Rawalpindi to Purshottam Das Anand who was born on 12th April 1896 at Rawalpindi. Purshottam Das Anand had completed college in Rawalpindi and was in the business of wholesale distribution of commodities. He thereafter expanded and opened a branch in Srinagar under the banner "Purshottam Das Anand and Sons". In 1935 he built a beautiful house in Gugji Bagh area of Srinagar. His base remained Rawalpindi from where he managed the business in Srinagar and Rawalpindi. A few years before the partition he shifted with family to Srinagar.

They had a comfortable life in Srinagar. Kashmir which was then a princely state and during partition had not chosen to join India or Pakistan. After independence in 1947 Pakistan invaded Kashmir and sent tribal militias from Waziristan to capture the princely state of Kashmir. The war was also known as the "First Kashmir War". The situation was not conducive for the family and the couple had no choice but to pack a few clothes and

leave Kashmir with their children. With no place of their own they stayed for a couple of years in Delhi, in Kanpur with Susheila's younger brother Narendra Nath Sethi, in Lucknow with her elder brother Amolak Ram Sethi and then bought a house on rent in Dehradun where they stayed till the situation stabilised in Kashmir and the daughters completed their education. Purshottam Das Anand had meanwhile moved back to Srinagar to revive his business.

Susheila (Sheila) and Purshottam Das Anand had two sons Satish and Sudhir (born on 15th Jan 1944) and 4 daughters Satya, Usha (born on 23rd March 1931), Pramila (Pimmi) born on 18th March 1933 and Harsh born on 16th August 1935.

Kulwant Rai Sethi – Harjas Rai Sethi – Sukhanand Sethi – Ram Krishan Sethi – Dani Ditta Lal Sethi – Narsingh Das Sethi – Ganesh Das Sethi – Chaman Lal Sethi

CHAMAN LAL SETHI

Chaman Lal Sethi was born on 23rd January 1908 and got married to Satya Kakkar in Rawalpindi. Chaman Lal Sethi and Satya had two sons Anil (born on 25th December 1940) and Arun (born on 10th December 1949) and three daughters Manjula (born on 20th September 1944), Reena (born on 6th December 1946) and Meenakshi (born on 20th December 1948).

Chaman Lal Sethi was a great revolutionary who was actively involved in the Indian freedom struggle since the age of 14. He left his studies mid-way while he was a student at Victoria Diamond Jubilee Technical Institute which enraged his elder brother Amolak Ram. Chaman Lal took a train to Rawalpindi without informing anyone and got further involved in the freedom struggle. He was jailed and tortured many times but did not give up. His experience and story of resilience during the freedom struggle is an interesting read and deserves a special place in this book on Sethi's. After partition he settled in Moradabad.

CHAMAN LAL SETHI – REVOLUTIONARY and FREEDOM FIGHTER

While going through the various manuscripts and writings of Shri Chaman Lal Sethi, I was deeply moved and filled with a sense of great pride. Having spent considerable time with him during my childhood and even during the 1970s I used to listen to him narrate various incidents of the freedom struggle, but it was only when I went through his writings that I truly got to know the hardships he went through during his days as a revolutionary for the freedom struggle of our country.

Chaman Lal Sethi documented his entire life using a 1930's *'brother' typewriter,* which has been preserved by his grandchildren.

It is not possible to include all his writings in this book, but I would like to share *'ad verbatim'*, the letter which he had written to the Home Secretary, Government of India, in response to the Home Secretary's letter to him for getting the freedom fighter's pension. This letter gives a glimpse of certain unknown facts about the history of the freedom struggle and the trials and tribulations which Chaman Lal Sethi underwent as a young man.

"In 1922 at the age of 14 years, I joined the Congress Volunteers Core and Khilafat movement and participated in the wine and other shop picketing programs of the Congress. I was beaten by the police and arrested twice for a term of week each. I took keen interest in the collection and burning of foreign clothes. While leading a children's procession during the visit of Lala Lajpat Rai in Rawalpindi, opposite the City Police Station, I was dragged in and given beatings and kicks and was released after four hours. I also worked actively in the salt making satyagraha movement and was awarded an 8-day term. I had also collected a good amount of money running in thousands for the TILAK SWARAJYA FUND.

From 1928 I joined the Kirti Kisan Sabha, Bharat Naujwan Sabha and the Republican Association Army, all revolutionary parties, and had my training in the use of firearms. I opened a General Store (Alma Stores) at U/595 Hans Lane, Rawalpindi so that members of the party could hold the meetings and chalk out the party programs. Six special CID men were put permanently to watch and follow me and the incoming persons to know their whereabouts and working of the party.

I participated in the Lahore Congress Session under the Presidentship of Pandit Jawahar Lal Nehru as an organizer of the Volunteers Corp (Sardar Mangal Singh as G.O.C.). One early morning the volunteers blackened the face of one C.I.D. officer, as the entry of police was prohibited on the campus. The situation became very tense with the police surrounding the campus from all sides and demanding the surrender of those 2 volunteers. Gandhiji immediately called me with Sardar Mangal Singh G.O.C.

In June 1930 I was arrested in the 2nd Lahore Conspiracy Case under various charges u/s 5and6 - Explosive Substances Act (Bomb Act), u/s 120 - Conspiracy against the Crown, u/s 17 - A member of an Unlawful Association and some other charges after a day long search of my house and store, wherein the police took away most of the stores articles, cash and manuscripts of the 1st Lahore Conspiracy Case which I had prepared for print with photos of Sardar Bhagat Singh, RajGuru, Principal Chhabil Das, Ram Chander B.A. (National) and others including the great martyr Jatinder Nath Das.

Immediately, I was taken into custody. The police arranged to cut off my nails from my hands and for the chemical test. This was in connection with the simultaneous Bomb explosions in Rawalpindi, Lahore, Gujranwala, Lyallpur and Amritsar that day.

I was sent to Jhanda thana police station where, by night, Bhai Shri Ram Chhibber of Vashnaghar, Gurbax Singh and Prahlad Dutt were also arrested and lodged in the cell to me. After 3 days I learnt that Shri Jagan Nath Kohli, our Naujwan Bharat Sabha Secretary was also detained. I was shifted to solitary police quarters near the Chaklala line after six days and locked in a small room with handcuffs tied to a charpai where 4 police and CID men were posted to interrogate and beat me. For the first seven days they did not let me sleep and whenever I felt sleepy, they would beat me by giving slaps, kicks in my stomach and pulling my hair. My bowels had not worked for six days and on the seventh day I fainted in the morning and regained consciousness in the evening.

Next morning I was taken to the police hospital where Doctor Tara Singh gave me Enema and some mixture. He also advised the S.S.P. to allow me to sleep as my condition was very alarming. A good number of police officers Mr. Beaty D.S.P., Sant Ram Kapur (Retired IG – CID, Railways), Bakshi Guranditta and other police officers were put on me for interrogation. They gave me good beating from time to time by hanging me with legs tied to the roof.

All my bail applications were rejected by the Sessions Judge and the High Court. Finally, a Habeas Corpus Petition presented by my elder brother Amolak Ram Sethi vs. Emperor was accepted by the High Court and my counsel Shri Dev Raj Sawhney, a barrister of Lahore and my relatives were allowed to meet me and provide me food and clothing (It has reference in 133-I.C. 1931-page 288 Habeas Corpus Application under section 491, criminal procedure case Lahore High Court, Criminal Miscellaneous No. 124 of 1930, July 1, 1930). This too was not carried till the orders of the Punjab Government.

Some time later my application for my transfer from Police custody to Judicial lock up was granted by Mr. Reid, the Sessions Judge who was reported about my serious condition in police custody due to regular brutal torture and practicing barbarous reprisals against me in contravention of all civilized legal norms.

To look into this inhuman treatment, the European Civil Surgeon who examined me in jail the following morning, recommended the D.I.G. Police to investigate my beatings by the police officers responsible. The D.I.G. then suspended and dismissed the six police officers. In the jail I was locked up in a solitary cell and nobody was allowed to see me. No food was served to me for 4 days in the jail.

On the 5th day two long term convicts, Kartar Singh, co-accused of Chaudhary Sher Jang of Malerkotla train robbery case and Nand Lal of Mughalpura wagons burning case supplied me jaggery and milk of which I had prepared milk lassi. That very night I suffered from Cholera when my room was under 3-4 ft. of water due to very heavy rain and storm that night.

While in jail I was produced before Sardar Hardyal Singh, City Magistrate, for being a member of an unlawful association. My legal counsel, Mr. Dev Raj Sawhney, Diwan Daulat Rai Sawhney and Mr. A. Jan, all Barristers of repute conducted my case, while the Crown was represented by Mr. R.B. Gopal Das, prosecuting Dy. S.P.

The city magistrate Sardar Hardyal Singh did not accept the plea that while in detention, long before the Naujwan Bharat Sabha was declared an unlawful association, I cannot be tried for this offence and after 2 hearings convicted and sentenced me to 6 months imprisonment.

The theft of a suitcase in the train by one of our workers, recovered by the police contained valuable information about our link and this made the police hands tight. The police had made several raids at my house and Stores during 1930-1931 and removed and stole valuable goods and thousands of rupees cash, suspected to be for the use of our party, as also the ornaments of my sister, which were never returned.

For the Karachi Congress Session when Gandhi-Irwin pact was to be voted, I was elected as a Congress Delegate from Rawalpindi leading the group of Late Diwan Chaman Lal Sawhney (MP), Lala Kanshi Ram Sethi, President City Congress Committee and Lala Gokal Chand Bhasin, Advocate.

When I was to leave for Karachi the very sad news of the execution of Sarvshri Bhagat Singh, Raj Guru and Sukhdev came. I led the historic procession with thousands of men, women and children to show our grief and sorrow. Every person in the city was shocked and in tears.

Sardar Vallabh Bhai Patel was the President of the Karachi Congress Session and Subhash Chandra Bose was the President of the Naujwan Bharat Sabha to oppose the Gandhi-Irwin pact. There was some trouble and confusion the night before the resolution was to be put to vote and Gandhi ji sent for us. Dr. Mohd. Alam, Barrister Sardar Bhag Singh, Ahmad Din Mansoor and I met Gandhiji at 11:00 in the night on behalf of the party, where Sardar Patel, Nehru ji and Shri Jamnalal Bajaj were also present. Gandhiji, with tears in his eyes, showed his sad feelings and mistake for the execution of the martyrs Bhagat Singh and his comrades. He admitted that their lives could have been saved if the matter was tackled by him in a different way with the Viceroy, Lord Irwin.

After the Bharat Naujwan Sabha session, we were invited by the Republican Association Army of India for further handling of Arms at Bombay, but this was dropped with the leak of the news to my Caretaker (C.I.D. man Nauroz Khan), who was deputed from Lahore to shadow me. Some traitor gave him this information, which Nauroz Khan told me himself.

When I reached Lahore from Karachi on my way to Rawalpindi, the ADM Rawalpindi, Sardar Uttam Singh had already issued my search and arrest warrants whether I came by road or rail. They thrice attempted at Lahore, Chaklala and Rawalpindi stations to search me, but fearing some armed conflict with my comrades and colleagues, who were also travelling with me, decided to search me at home without giving me any chance. They made the biggest raid with about 250 armed policemen at my house.

It was 4:30 in the morning of 4th April 1931. Our house was a big four storied building consisting of 15 living rooms besides many others. On my arrival home, I went to the top of the building. The police surrounded it from all sides a few minutes after my arrival there. My servant told me about the presence of police, and I rushed downstairs to check these people. I saw the ADM and City Magistrate with City Police Inspector Amat Nath near the stairs giving instructions to the policemen. I enquired about the purpose of their raid and told them that they can search the house and arrest me only when all the policemen are called out of the house after the search. They fell in my trap and for 15 minutes before the search began I talked with the City Magistrate Sardar Hardyal Singh, they laughed and joked with the ADM. In the meantime, during these fifteen minutes my younger sister and nephew had removed all that the police had come for. The search of the house went on till the afternoon and they were all surprised and disappointed to return empty-handed.

As written earlier, the traitor, our Joint Secretary, had passed on all information and our programs at Karachi to my caretaker, Nauroz Khan who had sent his report to the Government. Had I been caught this time the minimum imprisonment would have been a lifetime in jail as I had some arms and publications and orders from the H.Q., Republican Association Army of India.

We had planned to do away with our traitor, but the arrest of many of our comrades came in our way. By then the police had arrested most of the party members who were tried and sentenced to various terms of imprisonment.

Coincidentally, my mother had a very serious heart attack at home, the very night and time I had cholera in jail and her condition and health started deteriorating day by day. I then had to leave all my activities."

Kulwant Rai Sethi – Harjas Rai Sethi – Sukhanand Sethi – Ram Krishan Sethi – Dani Ditta Lal Sethi – Narsingh Das Sethi – Ganesh Das Sethi – Kaushalya Sethi

KAUSHALYA SETHI

Kaushalya was born on 25th December in Rawalpindi. She studied in Rawalpindi and got married to Mr. Roshan Lal Sabharwal in Rawalpindi.

Roshan Lal Sabharwal was born in Bhera. He was in the textile industry and worked in Lahore, Karachi, Madras, Poona, Bombay and Modi Nagar.

Kaushalya and Rohan Lal Sabharwal had three children, Uma (born on 8th January 1942), Anoop and Raksha (born on 12th September 1947).

Kulwant Rai Sethi – Harjas Rai Sethi – Sukhanand Sethi – Ram Krishan Sethi – Dani Ditta Lal Sethi – Narsingh Das Sethi – Ganesh Das Sethi – Raj Dulari Sethi

RAJ DULARI SETHI

Raj Dulari Sethi was born in Rawalpindi and got married at Lahore to Mr. Hans Raj Bhasin who was a leading timber merchant. After partition they migrated and settled at Ambala where Hans Raj Bhasin continued his business of Timber.

Raj Dulari and Hans Raj Bhasin had four sons, Daman (born in December 1936), Ashwini (born on 5th November 1940), Vijay (born on 24th February 1944), Vinay (born on 22nd December 1945) and Kamlesh (born on 8th September 1944)

Kulwant Rai Sethi – Harjas Rai Sethi – Sukhanand Sethi – Ram Krishan Sethi – Dani Ditta Lal Sethi – Narsingh Das Sethi – Ganesh Das Sethi – Narendra Nath Sethi

NARENDRA NATH SETHI

The youngest in the family, my father, Narendra Nath Sethi, was born on 3rd November 1919 and studied in Rawalpindi. He graduated in Law from Government College, Lahore.

A passionate horse rider, he co-owned several racehorses with his partner in Lahore, winning numerous derbies at the Lahore Racecourse. Some of the trophies won by his horses, including the Brunnhilde Cup, Mandalay Cup, and May Myo Cup, are still preserved.

Narendra Nath Sethi began his professional career in Lahore with Martin Burn and Co. Ltd. In early 1947, just months before Partition, he was transferred to Kanpur as Deputy Branch Manager. After Partition, his racehorse partner sold their horses and invited him to Lahore to collect his share. However, his eldest brother, Amolak Ram Sethi, strictly forbade him from going, as it was unsafe. Amolak, 25 years older than Narendra, had raised him like a son and was deeply protective of him.

Narendra Nath Sethi settled in "Murray Cottage" on Mall Road, Kanpur, which he rented from M/s. Murray and Co., owned by Mr. V.N. Singh, for Rs. 125 per month in September 1947. It was Mr. Singh's wife, Krishna, who introduced Narendra to her niece, Saroj Chopra, daughter of Mr. Hans Raj Chopra and Tara Chopra.

Narendra Sethi and Saroj Chopra were married in Dehradun, where Mr. Hans Raj Chopra was posted as Commissioner of Income Tax. Saroj's doli first arrived in Lucknow at the residence of Amolak Ram Sethi.

Saroj Sethi's father, Hans Raj Chopra, was a close friend of the renowned singer Kundan Lal Saigal. The two would often gather in the evenings, enjoying drinks while playing the harmonium and singing. The harmonium KL Saigal used was preserved by Saroj for decades before she donated it to the Ram Krishna Sharnam Trust when she left Kanpur for good in 2010.

Narendra Nath Sethi was an avid reader of Russian literature and maintained an extensive library on the Russian Revolution.

An extrovert by nature, he enjoyed entertaining friends both at home and at the Cawnpore Club.

Narendra Nath Sethi had a deep love for travel and would often take his family on road trips to Kashmir and other picturesque hill stations.

Tragically, he passed away on 1st September 1963 at the young age of 44, leaving behind three small children: myself, Rajiv (Bubli), then 10 years old (born on 6th February 1953) followed by Poonam, then 8 ½ years old (born on 24yj August 1954) and Rajat (Keetoo), just 5 years old (born on 28th February 1958).

Chaman Lal Sethi, his elder brother wrote in his memoirs

"I have few words to express for Bhabhi Saroj who was only 31 yrs old then and suffered so many difficulties and hardships at this young age and brought up her children so nicely." unquote.

Saroj Sethi was born on 22nd April 1932 in Shimla and studied at Queen Mary School, Delhi, where she actively participated in school plays. Married at the young age of 16, she later completed her graduation from S.N. Sen Degree College, Mall Road, Kanpur, after the death of her husband.

Following Narendra's passing, Saroj was unsure how to raise her three young children, but she had unwavering faith that the Almighty would guide her. Her Bhua's brother's daughter-in-law, Mrs. Mahendra Jit Singh, who worked at British India Corporation (BIC), asked Saroj to get clothes tailored for the 25th Anniversary of BIC's cotton mill, "Elgin Mills," for an exhibition and fashion show.

This marked the beginning of her passion for tailoring. When Elgin Mills later opened a retail showroom, she was appointed as its Manager.

Her journey was arduous, but through perseverance, she ensured the best education for her children and saw them well-settled in life. After retiring from Elgin Mills, she dedicated herself to social service, offering honorary work at the Spastic Centre in Kanpur to educate and empower children with disabilities.

Her 90th birthday was celebrated in grand style in Noida on 22nd April 2022, surrounded by her children, grandchildren and great-grandchildren.

Many of her relatives, friends, and loved ones attended her 90th birthday celebrations. On this special occasion, she released a coffee table book about her life, compiled by her children which also included her autobiography.

Now 93, she lives with her younger son, Rajat, in Noida. Though her memory is gradually fading, she still enjoys solving Sudoku puzzles daily and singing her favorite old songs beautifully.

Saroj Sethi with her children, grandchildren and grandson on her 90th birthday

NINTH GENERATION

1) **AMOLAK RAM SETHI and FAMILY**

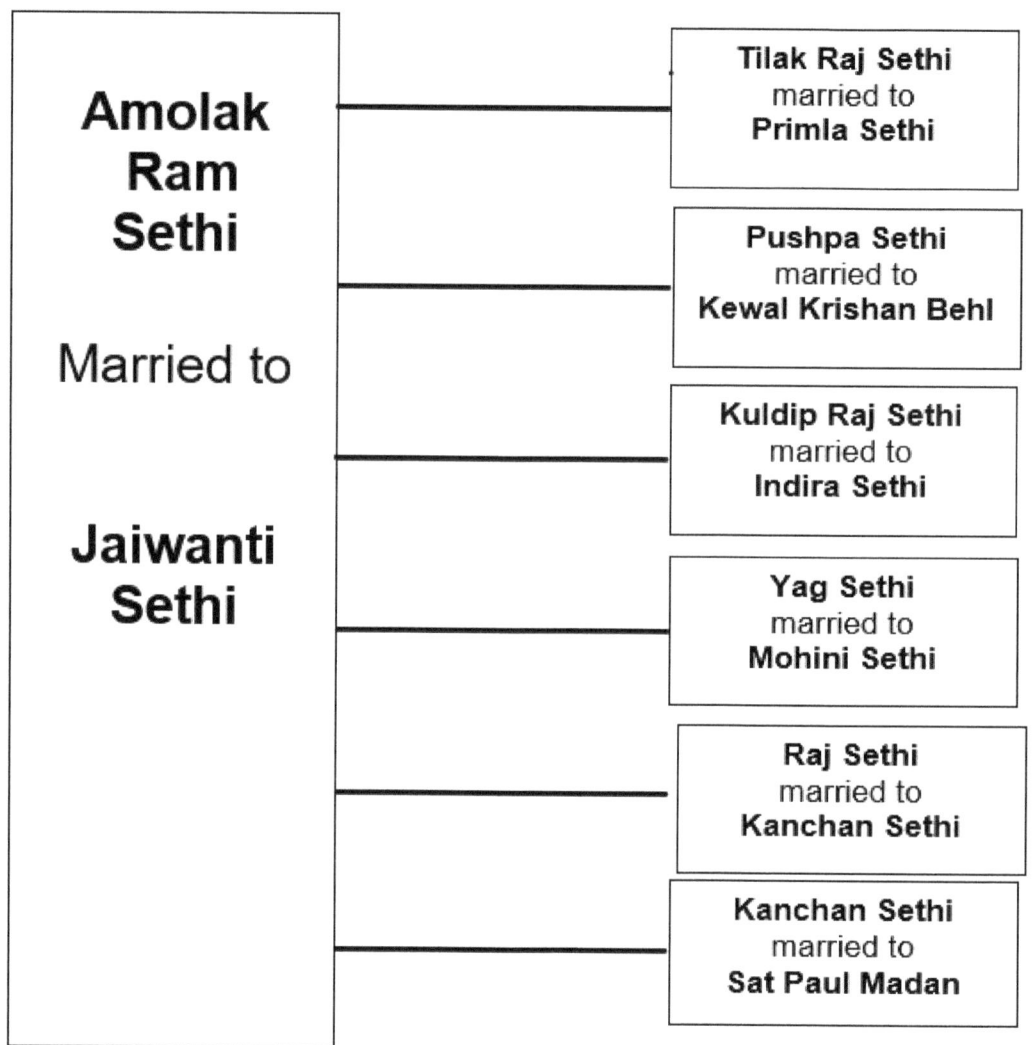

Kulwant Rai Sethi – Harjas Rai Sethi – Sukhanand Sethi – Ram Krishan Sethi – Dani Ditta Lal Sethi – Narsingh Das Sethi – Ganesh Das Sethi – Amolak Ram Sethi – Tilak Raj Sethi

TILAK RAJ SETHI

Tilak Raj Sethi was the eldest in the family of Amolak Ram Sethi. He was born on 8th March 1924 at Lahore.

His school and college (Government college) education were completed in Lahore after which he went to Loughborough University, UK, from where he did his Engineering.

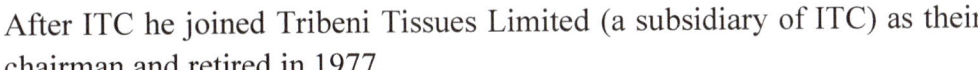

After his initial training at Imperial Tobacco Co., UK, Tilak Raj Sethi joined Indian Tobacco Co. in 1943 and was with them till 1973. During his long period of service with ITC he was posted all over India including Kanpur as the Region Head. He was thereafter posted in the head office at Calcutta where he spent the longest time.

After ITC he joined Tribeni Tissues Limited (a subsidiary of ITC) as their chairman and retired in 1977.

Tilak Raj Sethi married Primla on 22nd November 1949.

Primla was born on 22nd October 1929 in Kashmir. During her younger days she was an ace tennis player. After marriage she took to playing Bridge and excelled in the same. While in Calcutta she took to Interior decoration and flower arrangement and was well known in the corporate sector. An excellent cook, her cooking expertise was known far and wide and always kept a good table and was extremely house proud. She loved to travel and enjoyed adventure.

Tilak Raj Sethi and Primla were doting parents to their three boys – Sanjay Sethi (born on 16th August 1951), Ajay Sethi (born on 4th June 1957) and Vijay Sethi (born on 2nd November 1963).

Kulwant Rai Sethi – Harjas Rai Sethi – Sukhanand Sethi – Ram Krishan Sethi – Dani Ditta Lal Sethi – Narsingh Das Sethi – Ganesh Das Sethi – Amolak Ram Sethi – Pushpa Sethi

PUSHPA SETHI

Pushpa Sethi, the 2nd child of Amolak Ram Sethi and Jaiwanti was born on 23rd November 1925 at Lahore.

She did her schooling at Lahore and got married to Kewal Krishan Behl (born on 11th January 1921) on 23rd February 1943 at Lahore.

After the partition of the country, they shifted to Lucknow where Kewal Krishan Behl started restaurants. He was also involved with the Stock Exchange and used to often visit Bombay.

Pushpa Behl (Sethi) meanwhile was busy bringing up the children Chittranjan (born on 10th September 1944 at Lahore), Neelima (born on 22nd November 1946), Rajiv (born on 10th May 1948), Vipin (born on 20th August 1950) and Neeta born on 4th September 1952).

Kulwant Rai Sethi – Harjas Rai Sethi – Sukhanand Sethi – Ram Krishan Sethi – Dani Ditta Lal Sethi – Narsingh Das Sethi – Ganesh Das Sethi – Amolak Ram Sethi – Kuldip Raj Sethi

KULDIP RAJ SETHI

Kuldip Raj Sethi was born on 4th May 1929 and qualified as a mechanical Engineer. He spent 10 years in U.K. and returned to India and joined 'Metal Box' and thereafter joined Heavy Engineering Corporation in Ranchi. The government then sent him to Czechoslovakia for one year.

Kuldip Raj Sethi got married to Indira on 15th October 1961.

Indira was a teacher and later became the head of her school in Ranchi.

Kuldip Raj Sethi and Indira were very caring persons with high principles.

Since they had no children, they adopted their helper's daughter and ensured that she got the best education and got settled in life and willed a large part of their property and assets to them.

Kulwant Rai Sethi – Harjas Rai Sethi – Sukhanand Sethi – Ram Krishan Sethi – Dani Ditta Lal Sethi – Narsingh Das Sethi – Ganesh Das Sethi – Amolak Ram Sethi – Yag Sethi

YAG SETHI

Yag Sethi was born on 26th July 1933 at Lahore and completed his studies at Lucknow.

Yag Sethi started his career with "Fiat" that sent him to Italy for training in Automobile Engineering at their headquarters in Turin. He later joined "Dunlop" and rose to the position of Regional Manager (W) posted at Bombay. While with Dunlop Yag Sethi was posted across the country in Lucknow, Nagpur, Ahmedabad, Calcutta, Hyderabad, Delhi and Bombay. After his long stint with Dunlop, he joined J.K. Tyres as their Regional Manager (N) at Delhi.

Yag Sethi married Mohini on 17th January 1958 at Lucknow. Mohini was born on 10th March 1937 at Rawalpindi and did her schooling at Bhartiya Balika Vidyalaya, Lucknow, where classes were conducted in the open. She recalls that she always wore a white salwar kameez and dupatta. She later graduated with the Bachelor of Arts degree from S.N. Sen Degree College, Mall Road, Kanpur.

Yag and Mohini's first meeting is an interesting story, and this is how his sister Kanchan narrates it:

"YAG bhapa and Mohini's is a long saga. Briefly,

I dialled a friend's number, and got this strange voice, obviously a wrong number. This voice said since you have the connection why don't we speak to each other! At the end of conversation, this person gave her name Mohini and said we should talk to each other again. We had to exchange correct telephone numbers, as the connection was a wrong number!

After few months of occasional phone conversations, it was decided a meeting would be good. The only way I could meet a stranger was if my brother took me. YAG bhapa thought it not a good idea to meet a stranger, but reluctantly agreed on condition that it would be for maximum 5 mins.

Mohini lived in an apartment above Capitol cinema in Lucknow. I asked her to meet me by the car. There emerged this knock me down most attractive girl. We spoke for few minutes and as I turned to get in the car my dear brother said there was no rush!

Then YAG bhapa was very keen I meet up with Mohini again. It was a mutual attraction as YAG bhapa was a handsome young man and Mohini was extremely beautiful.

Life became complicated for them, as Mohini's father got transferred to Kanpur. In the meantime, I got married and came to England. YAG bhapa spent a year training in Italy.

When the marriage question arose, Papaji wrote to me to ask about Mohini and YAG bhapa. So that is when YAG bhapa said he was keen to marry Mohini. Happy ending to a story with many ups and downs. As my mother Maji would say "Sanjog".

All because I dialled a wrong number!! How good was that. Our paths would never have crossed, as we went to different schools and families and were not in the same social circle."

After meeting Mohini, Yag Sethi got a "bodyguard" to watch over her. Ganesh, a close friend of Yag Sethi would beat the hell out of anyone who even dared to look in her direction.

Mohini had a great passion for baking and cooking. During the period when they were in Calcutta Mohini was encouraged by her sister-in-law, Pramila (wife of Tilak Raj Sethi) to take it up as a profession.

Mohini, started in a small way by taking orders from the residents of their building. With much apprehension and nervousness but with huge support and encouragement from her husband she started cooking classes which proved to be a great hit. Since then, she has never looked back and has expanded her hobby and passion into a thriving business taking catering orders. Many of the ladies would pass off her scrumptious cakes and desserts as their own creations much to Mohini's amusement.

After Yag Sethi retired they moved to their own home in Faridabad where Mohini continued with her baking and cooking venture and became very popular in Delhi and Faridabad. She was also featured with her creations in a newspaper which commented **"Even at 74 Mohini Sethi can work for 10 hours a day without any assistance"**.

Yag and Mohini were parents to their doting children Amita Sethi (born on 9th November 1958), Kapil Sethi (born on 26th April 1963) and Anil Sethi (born on 2nd January 1965).

Mohini Sethi presently lives in New Friends Colony, New Delhi close to her daughter Amita's home.

Recently on 27th March 2025 at the age of 89, Mohini Sethi penned a memory of hers, which in her own handwriting appears below:

मेरे Father in law का नाम अमरनाथ राम था उनके छोटे भाई का नाम नरिन्द्र uncle था उनकी wife का नाम सरोज चाची जी थी । सरोज चाची जी elgin mill में काम करती थी । नरिन्द्र uncle की death छोटी उम्र में हो गई थी ।

सरोज aunty के 2 लड़के और 1 लड़की है - राजीव सेठी, रजत सेठी और बेटी का नाम पूनम सेठी ।

मेरे father G.L. Luthra था - जबकि नाम भूपाट । मेरे father और नरिन्द्र नरिन्द्र uncle, ताऊ खेला करते थे together मेरे बड़ा होने की - मुझे सरोज चाची जी walk करते भाले थे भी मेरे की बड़ी याद से साथ लेकर जाया करते थे - walk करते काले छप्पन से भी भाई से - मुझे याद है कि नरिन्द्र uncle की शादी में मैं गई थी

Kulwant Rai Sethi – Harjas Rai Sethi – Sukhanand Sethi – Ram Krishan Sethi – Dani Ditta Lal Sethi – Narsingh Das Sethi – Ganesh Das Sethi – Amolak Ram Sethi – Raj Sethi

RAJ SETHI

Raj Sethi was born on 12th September 1935 at Lahore. He studied at London School of Economics, U.K. and started his career with Escorts Limited at Faridabad.

Raj Sethi married Kanchan Sethi on 11th December 1963 at Delhi. Kanchan Sethi (Mani) was born on 8th October 1944 at Peshawar.

Raj Sethi and Kanchan Sethi have three daughters, Shalini (born on 6th July 1966, Malini (born on 14th November 1967 and Ragini (born on 10th October 1970).

Kulwant Rai Sethi – Harjas Rai Sethi – Sukhanand Sethi – Ram Krishan Sethi – Dani Ditta Lal Sethi – Narsingh Das Sethi – Ganesh Das Sethi – Amolak Ram Sethi – Kanchan Sethi

KANCHAN SETHI (MADAN)

Kanchan Sethi was born on 31st August 1938 at Lahore. Since her parents had shifted to Lucknow before partition, Kanchan did her schooling at La Martiniere Girls School, Lucknow.

Kanchan Sethi got married on 24th February 1957 to Sat Paul Madan in Lucknow and after marriage settled in U.K. where she brought up her three children and worked part time checking NHS forms.

Kanchan was heavily involved in voluntary work and ran the hospital patient's library. Kanchan has the rare distinction of being a magistrate for 27 years.

Sat Paul Madan was born on 29th August 1930 at Quetta, which is the capital of Baluchistan. His father was a doctor who had devoted his life in helping and treating the poor. After partition the family moved to Delhi. Satya qualified as a dental surgeon and worked in Calcutta and then moved to London and practised at 'Guys Hospital'.

They presently live in U.K. and are proud parents to three children, Meeka (born on 25th August 1958), Ira (born on 7th November 1961) and Savi Raj (born on 20th March 1965).

2) **LAKHWANTI SETHI (SAWHNEY) and FAMILY**

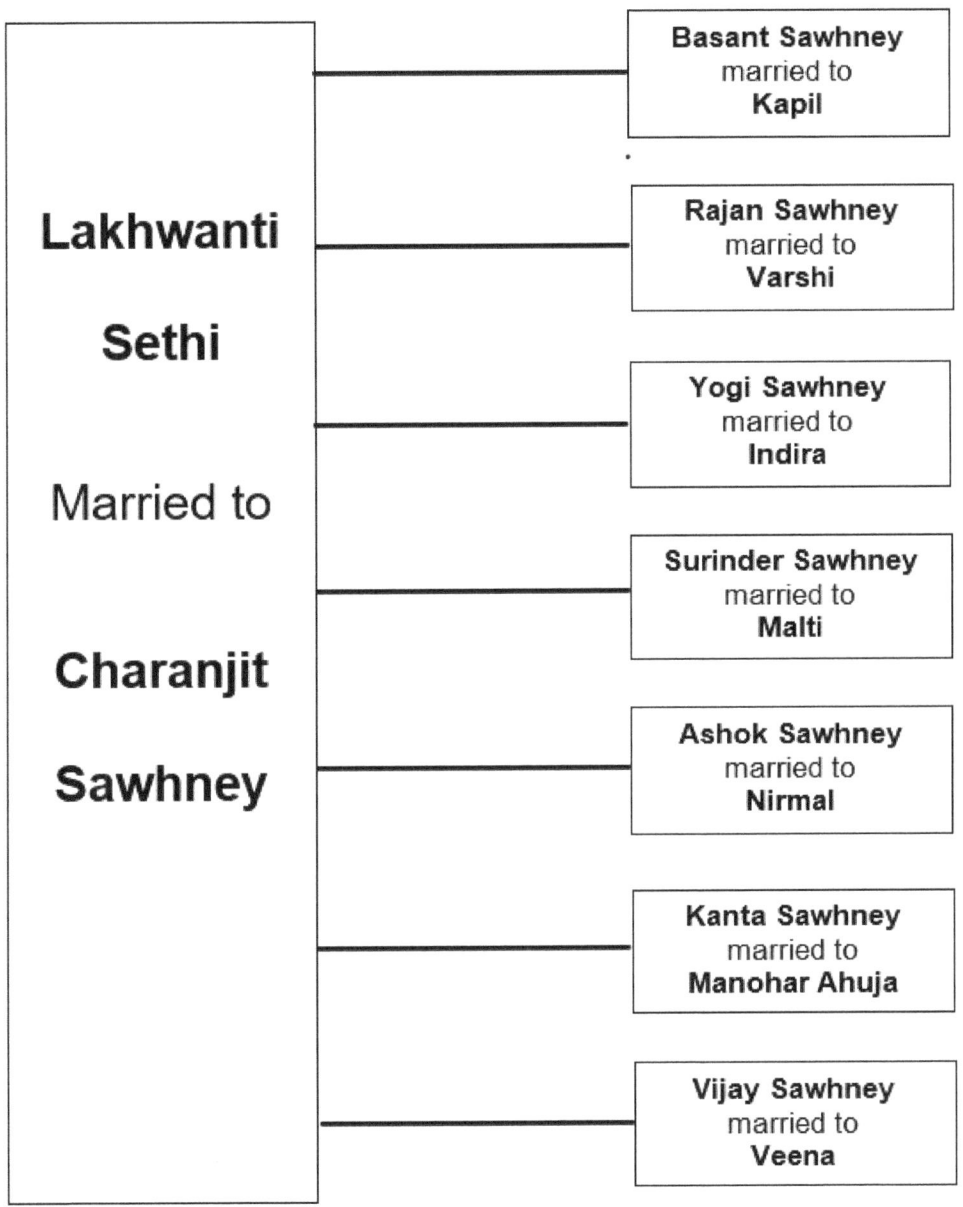

Kulwant Rai Sethi – Harjas Rai Sethi – Sukhanand Sethi – Ram Krishan Sethi – Dani Ditta Lal Sethi – Narsingh Das Sethi – Ganesh Das Sethi – Lakhwanti Sethi – Basant Sawhney

BASANT SAWHNEY

Basant was born at Bhera in 1920. She got married in 1946 at Rawalpindi to Om Prakash Kapil who was a Garrison Engineer with the Indian Army.

He was posted at various places including Jammu and later settled in Jalandhar.

Basant did her schooling in Rawalpindi and after marriage started teaching. She retired as the Principal of Arya Girls College, Jalandhar.

Their children, Gautam and Kanchan are settled in USA and the youngest Vikram is settled in Jalandhar.

Kulwant Rai Sethi – Harjas Rai Sethi – Sukhanand Sethi – Ram Krishan Sethi – Dani Ditta Lal Sethi – Narsingh Das Sethi – Ganesh Das Sethi – Lakhwanti Sethi – Rajan Sawhney

RAJAN SAWHNEY

Rajan Sawhney was born on 24th September 1923 in Rawalpindi and completed his schooling and college at Rawalpindi.

He worked with the Transport Department of Punjab and Haryana and during his tenure was posted at Amritsar, Ambala and Chandigarh. Rajan Sawhney retired as the Transport Commissioner of Haryana Roadways and settled in Chandigarh.

Rajan Sawhney was married to Dr. Varshi who was born on 20th September 1926i, Rajan Sawhney and Dr. Varshi Sawhney had two sons, Sanjeev Sawhney and Rajeev Sawhney.

Kulwant Rai Sethi – Harjas Rai Sethi – Sukhanand Sethi – Ram Krishan Sethi – Dani Ditta Lal Sethi – Narsingh Das Sethi – Ganesh Das Sethi – Lakhwanti Sethi – Surinder Sawhney

SURINDER SAWHNEY

Surinder Sawhney was born on 24th December 1929 at Rawalpindi.

He completed his schooling from Rawalpindi and did his graduation from Meerut. He got married to Malti on 22nd October 1966.

During his long tenure of over 35 years with Ceat Tyres, Surinder was posted at Mumbai, Delhi, Jaipur, Jodhpur, Agra, Kanpur and finally at Jorhat in Assam when he retired. In the year 2000 they shifted to Delhi.

Malti was born on 12th September 1943 in Hoshiarpur and completed her studies there. Malti's father, Ram Prakash Ohri was a renowned Urdu poet and 'shayar', also known as 'Sahir Hoshiarpuri'.

Having the genes of a poet, Malti herself is a wonderful poet and 'shayar' and has participated in many "Mushairas".

During their posting at Agra, as a hobby, Malti ventured into the 'beauty' business and when posted at Kanpur she took it up as a profession and opened her own Beauty Salon (Eve's Beauty Parlour). Since then, she never looked back and is running her salon in Gurgaon.

Surinder and Malti have three children, Ritu (born on 9th August 1967), Vishal (born on 15th August 1970) and Ruchi (born on 5th December 1973).

Kulwant Rai Sethi – Harjas Rai Sethi – Sukhanand Sethi – Ram Krishan Sethi – Dani Ditta Lal Sethi – Narsingh Das Sethi – Ganesh Das Sethi – Lakhwanti Sethi – Yogi Sawhney

YOGI SAWHNEY

Yogi Sawhney was born in Rawalpindi on 1st January 1928. He completed his studies from Banaras Hindu University, Varanasi and worked as a Jr. Scientific Officer in the Electronics department. He later joined Civil Defence in Dehradun and was later transferred to Bangalore. Yogi Sawhney got married to Indra on 30th June 1947. Indra worked with the Defence department and was one of the first women to be recruited in Civil Defence prior to the 1965 war.

Indra now lives in Bangalore. They have a daughter named Kirti.

Kulwant Rai Sethi – Harjas Rai Sethi – Sukhanand Sethi – Ram Krishan Sethi – Dani Ditta Lal Sethi – Narsingh Das Sethi – Ganesh Das Sethi – Lakhwanti Sethi – Ashok Sawhney

ASHOK SAWHNEY

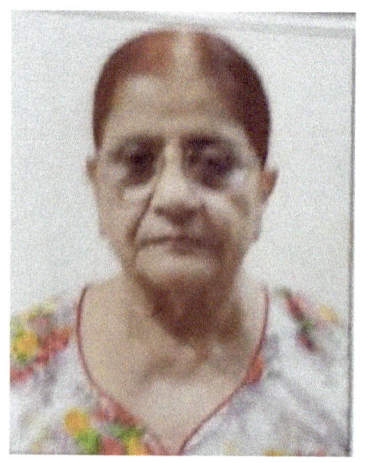

Ashok Sawhney was born in Rawalpindi on 25th July 1932 and finished his studies there. He did his graduation from Dehradun and started his career with UP Roadways, being posted at various places. His last posting was as The Regional Manager, UPSRTC at Agra.

On 7th May 1963 Ashok Sawhney married Nirmal at Jullundur.

Ashok Sawhney died on 26th February 1992. Indra Sawhney now lives in Agra.

They have three daughters, Nidhi, Anju and Vibha.

Kulwant Rai Sethi – Harjas Rai Sethi – Sukhanand Sethi – Ram Krishan Sethi – Dani Ditta Lal Sethi – Narsingh Das Sethi – Ganesh Das Sethi – Lakhwanti Sethi – Vijay Sawhney

VIJAY SAWHNEY

Vijay Sawhney was born in Patna on 25th December 1935.

He completed his B. Tech (Textiles) from BITS, Bhiwani.

Vijay Sawhney worked in the textile industry stationed at Ahmedabad, Chandigarh and Indore. He retired as the Director (Technical) of National Textile Corporation at Indore.

His expertise was instrumental in the modernization of textile operations.

Vijay Sawhney married Veena on 8th May 1963 at Jalandhar and settled in Indore. Veena was born on 25th June 1941 at Jalandhar. She studied at Arya Kanya Maha Vidyalaya, Delhi and did her B.A.(Hons.) in English from Indraprastha College, Delhi.

Veena is the Founder and President of Punjabi Mahila Vikas Samiti, M.P. and has made significant contribution towards women empowerment with over 35 clubs spread over entire Madhya Pradesh.

Her birthday 25th June is celebrated as 'Punjabi Diwas' in M.P. She presently lives in Indore. Vijay and Veena have two sons, Vivek and Vikas.

Kulwant Rai Sethi – Harjas Rai Sethi – Sukhanand Sethi – Ram Krishan Sethi – Dani Ditta Lal Sethi – Narsingh Das Sethi – Ganesh Das Sethi – Lakhwanti Sethi – Kanta Sawhney

KANTA SAWHNEY

Kanta Sawhney was born on August 14, 1933, in Rawalpindi. She completed her early education there and, following the Partition, pursued postgraduate studies in Jalandhar, earning an M.A. in English Literature.

On May 18, 1956, she married Manohar Lal Ahuja in Ambala.

Manohar Lal Ahuja was born on September 26, 1929, in Dera Ismail Khan, now part of Pakistan.

He obtained a B.A. in English (Honors) from

Lahore and later earned a B.E. in Electrical Engineering from Jabalpur. Manohar Lal Ahuja went on to serve as Chief Engineer of the Madhya Pradesh Electricity Board.

Manohar Lal Ahuja passed away on October 21, 1985, and Kanta Ahuja on March 26, 2011.

Together, they had three sons: Pankaj, Ambuj, and Anuj.

Kulwant Rai Sethi – Harjas Rai Sethi – Sukhanand Sethi – Ram Krishan Sethi – Dani Ditta Lal Sethi – Narsingh Das Sethi – Ganesh Das Sethi – Lajwanti Sethi

3) LAJWANTI SETHI

Lajwanti Sethi died at a very young age and was not married.

Kulwant Rai Sethi – Harjas Rai Sethi – Sukhanand Sethi – Ram Krishan Sethi – Dani Ditta Lal Sethi – Narsingh Das Sethi – Ganesh Das Sethi – Dina Nath Sethi

4) DINA NATH SETHI and FAMILY

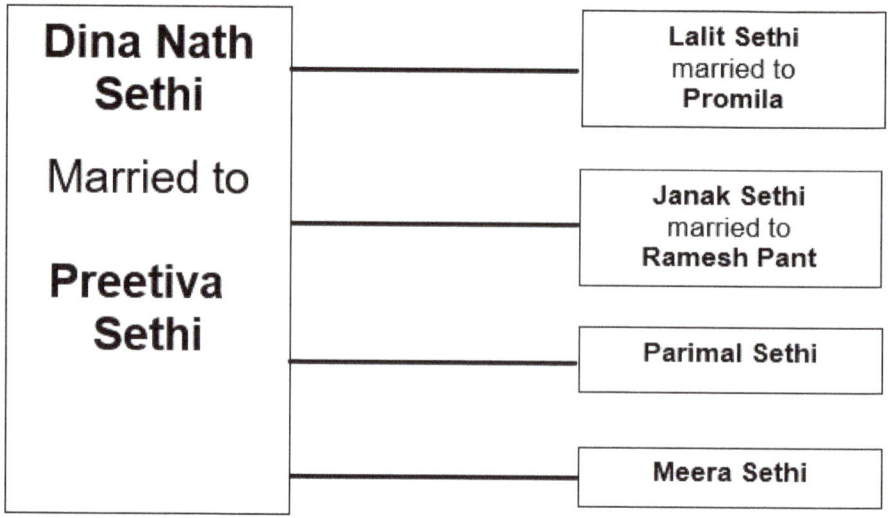

Kulwant Rai Sethi – Harjas Rai Sethi – Sukhanand Sethi – Ram Krishan Sethi – Dani Ditta Lal Sethi – Narsingh Das Sethi – Ganesh Das Sethi – Dina Nath Sethi – Lalit Sethi

LALIT SETHI

Lalit Sethi was married to Promila, and they lived in Bareilly.

Kulwant Rai Sethi – Harjas Rai Sethi – Sukhanand Sethi – Ram Krishan Sethi – Dani Ditta Lal Sethi – Narsingh Das Sethi – Ganesh Das Sethi – Dina Nath Sethi – Janak Sethi

JANAK SETHI (PANT)

Janak Sethi was born on 24th October 1930. After completing her studies and her post graduation She joined as a professor in the Education department at Lucknow University.

Janak Sethi got married on 20th November 1964 to Mr. Ramesh Chand Pant an IAS officer who also was the District Magistrate of Lucknow.

After his successful stint as the District Magistrate of Lucknow, Ramesh Pant was appointed as the Director of the Administrative Training Institute in Nainital.

Thereafter, he was appointed as The Director of Information Services for the state of Uttar Pradesh.

After his retirement Ramesh Pant and Janak Pant continued to live in Lucknow.

Janak and Ramesh Pant have a daughter Vandana (Vannu), who carries on the legacy of this part of the family. She is a Healthcare Executive and lives in the San Francisco Bay Area, USA.

Janak left for her heavenly abode on 21st May 2023.

Kulwant Rai Sethi – Harjas Rai Sethi – Sukhanand Sethi – Ram Krishan Sethi – Dani Ditta Lal Sethi – Narsingh Das Sethi – Ganesh Das Sethi – Dina Nath Sethi – Parimal Sethi

PARIMAL SETHI

Capt. Parimal Sethi (Pimmi) was in the merchant navy and before retirement was the Commander in Shipping Corporation of India.

Parimal Sethi had travelled widely and chose to remain a bachelor. After his retirement he settled in Lucknow with his mother and sister Meera Sethi (Cuckoo).

Parimal Sethi left for his heavenly abode from his home in Lucknow.

Kulwant Rai Sethi – Harjas Rai Sethi – Sukhanand Sethi – Ram Krishan Sethi – Dani Ditta Lal Sethi – Narsingh Das Sethi – Ganesh Das Sethi – Dina Nath Sethi – Meera Sethi

MEERA SETHI

Meera Sethi fondly called by all as Cuckoo was the youngest.

Meera Sethi was born on 8th August 1940 and studied at Rampur and Bareilly.

After her post graduation she settled in Lucknow with her mother and brother Parimal Sethi.

Meera Sethi joined the Loreto Girls Degree college (later named as Avadh Girls Degree college), Lucknow as a Librarian and continued as the Librarian till her retirement.

Meera Sethi (Cuckoo) left for her heavenly abode on 25th July 2023.

Kulwant Rai Sethi – Harjas Rai Sethi – Sukhanand Sethi – Ram Krishan Sethi – Dani Ditta Lal Sethi – Narsingh Das Sethi – Ganesh Das Sethi – Susheila Sethi

5) SUSHEILA SETHI (ANAND) and FAMILY

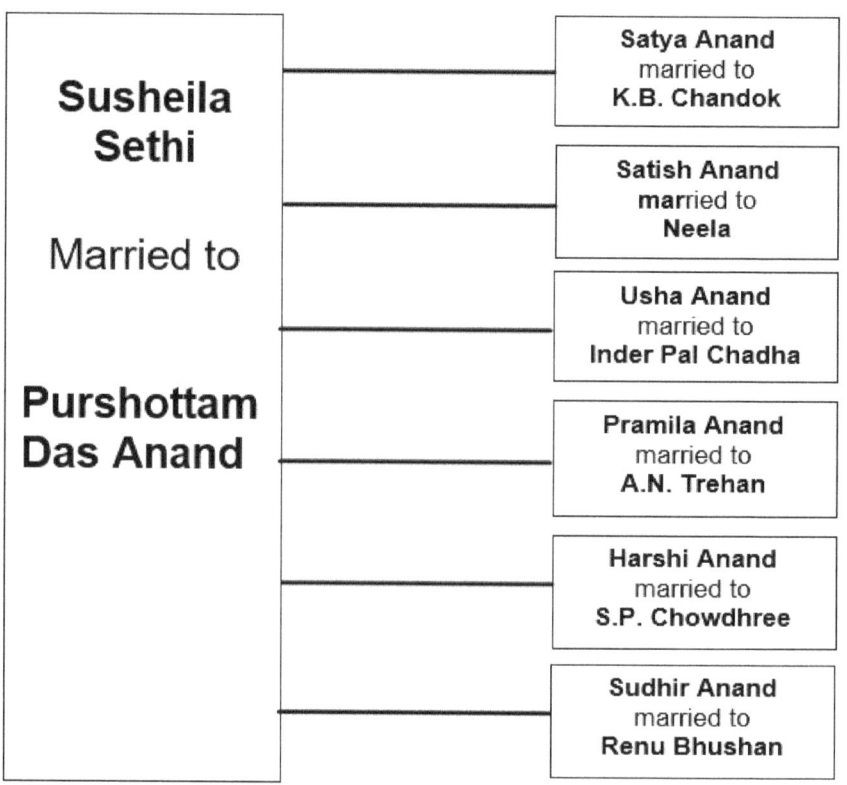

Kulwant Rai Sethi – Harjas Rai Sethi – Sukhanand Sethi – Ram Krishan Sethi – Dani DittaLal Sethi – Narsingh Das Sethi – Ganesh Das Sethi - Susheila Sethi – Satya Anand

SATYA ANAND

Satya Anand was the eldest and was born at Rawalpindi. She completed her schooling from Rawalpindi.

Satya Anand got married to K.B. Chandok from Lahore.

K.B. Chandok had his schooling and college in Lahore. He started dealing in Automobile parts and over the years the business grew and their firm 'The Upper India Trading Co. Pvt. Limited' set up its branches at Madras and Bombay. After partition they shifted to Madras and later settled in Bombay and became leaders in Automobile parts.

Satya and K.B. Chandok had two children, namely, Navin (born on 28th January 1945 at Lahore) and Anju (born on 4th November 1946 in Madras)

Kulwant Rai Sethi – Harjas Rai Sethi – Sukhanand Sethi – Ram Krishan Sethi – Dani Ditta Lal Sethi – Narsingh Das Sethi – Ganesh Das Sethi – Susheila Sethi – Satish Anand

SATISH ANAND

Satish Anand was born at Rawalpindi and did his schooling at Rawalpindi and Srinagar. He met his future wife Neela while studying in USA. Neela, who was from Ahmedabad, was also a student there.

Satish and Neela got married in Los Angeles, USA and after living in USA for some years shifted to Bombay where Satish Anand started a business of Plastic Chemicals under the banner of 'Plastichemicals Pvt. Limited' and set up branches at Calcutta and Delhi with the Head office at Bombay.

They further expanded and set up 'Farrel Anand and Co.' and had a manufacturing unit at Ambernath, near Bombay manufacturing chemicals for the plastic and rubber Industry.

Satish and Neela had two children, Anil and Meera.

Kulwant Rai Sethi – Harjas Rai Sethi – Sukhanand Sethi – Ram Krishan Sethi – Dani Ditta Lal Sethi – Narsingh Das Sethi – Ganesh Das Sethi – Susheila Sethi – Usha Anand

USHA ANAND

Usha Anand was born at Rawalpindi on 23rd March 1931. She did her initial schooling at Rawalpindi and Srinagar and completed her graduation from D.A.V. College, Dehradun.

Usha Anand got married to Inder Pal Chadha on 19th November 1954 at Delhi. Inderpal Chadha was born on 22nd October 1926 at Ichhra near Lahore in the province of Punjab where his father had an ice factory. Inderpal studied at Lahore. After their marriage Usha and Inderpal settled in Delhi and Inderpal started the family business of Ice factory. Later he expanded into the business of distribution and became a distributor for various companies.

Usha continues to live in Delhi. Usha and Inderpal Chadha have a daughter, Mamta (born on 13th February 1959).

Kulwant Rai Sethi – Harjas Rai Sethi – Sukhanand Sethi – Ram Krishan Sethi – Dani Ditta Lal Sethi – Narsingh Das Sethi – Ganesh Das Sethi – Susheila Sethi – Pramila Anand

PRAMILA ANAND

Pramila (Pimmi) was born on 18th March 1933 at Rawalpindi. She studied in Rawalpindi and Srinagar and graduated from Dehradun.

On 26th January 1961 Pramila got married to Ajudhiya Nath Trehan at Delhi. A.N. Trehan was born on 16th March 1926 in the Gujarat region (now in Pakistan).

A.N. Trehan completed his studies in Lahore and after marriage they settled in Delhi.

A.N. Trehan was in the business of manufacturing Oxygen. His firm, 'Bharat Oxygen', was the largest manufacturer of Oxygen in Northern India.

Pramila and Ajudhiya Nath Trehan have a daughter, Aarti who was born on 3rd December 1968 at Delhi.

Kulwant Rai Sethi – Harjas Rai Sethi – Sukhanand Sethi – Ram Krishan Sethi – Dani Ditta Lal Sethi – Narsingh Das Sethi – Ganesh Das Sethi – Susheila Sethi – Harsh Anand

HARSH ANAND

Harsh Anand was born in Srinagar on 16th August 1935. Her parents had just completed building their house in Srinagar in 1935 when Harsh was born. She did her schooling in Srinagar and Dehradun and thereafter studied medicine from Lady Hardinge Medical College, Delhi and specialised in Child health.

She was attached to Kalavati Hospital in Delhi and was a professor in Srinagar Medical College.

Dr. Harsh Anand got married at Delhi on 17th May to S.P. Chowdhree who was an officer with the Indian Army and retired as a Colonel (both deceased).

After marriage they settled in Delhi where Dr. Harsh Chowdhree had a clinic in the Munirka area.

Kulwant Rai Sethi – Harjas Rai Sethi – Sukhanand Sethi – Ram Krishan Sethi – Dani Ditta Lal Sethi – Narsingh Das Sethi – Ganesh Das Sethi – Susheila Sethi – Sudhir Anand

SUDHIR ANAND

Sudhir Anand is the youngest of the Anand's and was born on 15th January 1944 at Rawalpindi. Sudhir had his early education at CMS Tinder Bisco School, Srinagar and thereafter graduated from Amar Singh College, Srinagar.

Sudhir started working with his elder brother Satish in the business of Plastic Chemicals. As a young boy in 1965 Sudhir used to cycle from Bombay to Ambernath to attend to his work at the manufacturing plant of 'ALA Chemicals' for a meagre salary of Rs. 250/=. While with A.L.A. Chemicals Sudhir handled the affairs of the company in Calcutta, Delhi and Bombay.

Over the years Sudhir settled in Bombay and became the Director of 'Farell Anand' and was involved with the company's liaison with the government. He set up his own unit for manufacturing chemicals for the rubber and plastic industry in Ambernath under the banner "Purshottam Das and Sons'.

He had the distinction of being appointed as The Chairman of The Rubber Machinery Division in 'AIEI' and CII.

On 6th October 1973 Sudhir married Renu Bhushan at Karnal. Renu is the daughter of Col. Vinya Bhushan and Rajeshwari Bhushan. Born on 19th October 1951 at Nilokheri, Dist. Karnal, Renu did her schooling at Jhansi, Srinagar, Karnal and graduated from G.C.W., Chandigarh.

After her marriage Renu attended a chocolate making class and got hooked to making chocolates. She improvised and started making chocolates in the 1980s as a hobby catering to friends.

The word spread and Renu was flooded with orders after she was featured in 'Bombay Times' as *"Chocolate Wali Aunty"* She got moulds from across the world and started making chocolates in all shapes and sizes. Renu Anand aptly named her chocolate brand as *"My Own Chocolates"*.

Many companies like Cathay Pacific, Command Cell phone, S. Kumars, Cinevista and Reliance Industries got chocolates made in the shape of their logos from her and used to order gift hampers for various festivals.

Cathay Pacific used to serve her chocolates to Business class passengers. On her 40th birthday, Tina Ambani ordered chocolates from Renu Anand. Later She opened an outlet in the Fort area of Mumbai which proved to be a grand success.

Sudhir Anand and Renu Bhushan Anand are settled in Bombay and have two sons, Sachin and Tarun.

Kulwant Rai Sethi – Harjas Rai Sethi – Sukhanand Sethi – Ram Krishan Sethi – Dani Ditta Lal Sethi – Narsingh Das Sethi – Ganesh Das Sethi – Chaman Lal Sethi

6) CHAMAN LAL SETHI and FAMILY

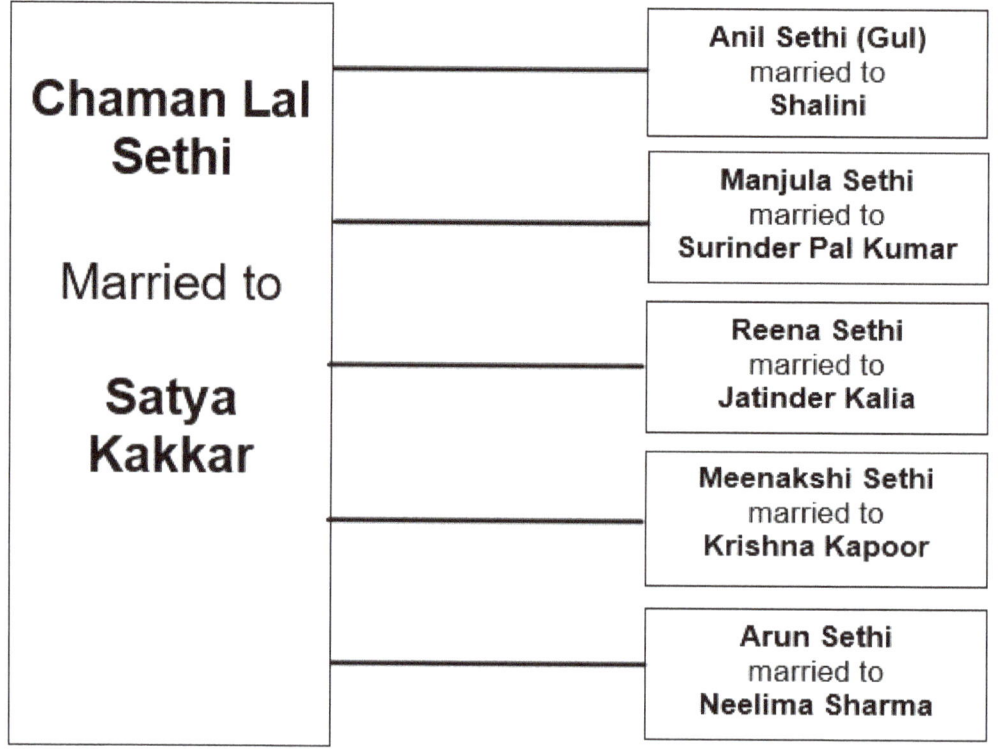

Kulwant Rai Sethi – Harjas Rai Sethi – Sukhanand Sethi – Ram Krishan Sethi – Dani Ditta Lal Sethi – Narsingh Das Sethi – Ganesh Das Sethi – Chaman Lal Sethi – Anil Sethi

ANIL SETHI (GUL)

Anil Sethi (Gul) was born in Rawalpindi on 25th December 1940. He studies at Rampur and Calcutta.

Anil started his career as an Air Conditioning Engineer with Arco Refrigeration Ltd., Bombay and after a few years went to Kuwait where he worked as an Air Conditioning Engineer.

Due to the turmoil in Kuwait Anil shifted to Bombay and worked with CIFCO Investments. During his tenure with Arco Refrigeration Ltd. In Bombay, Anil Sethi met Shalini Haldipure who was working in the same organisation as the Sales Head and they got married on 30th January 1974 at Chandigarh.

Shalini was born on 16th March 1941 at Bombay and had graduated from Wilson College, Bombay. After the sad demise of Shalini, Anil Sethi permanently shifted to Bhopal where he presently lives close to his sister Manjula's house.

Kulwant Rai Sethi – Harjas Rai Sethi – Sukhanand Sethi – Ram Krishan Sethi – Dani Ditta Lal Sethi – Narsingh Das Sethi – Ganesh Das Sethi – Chaman Lal Sethi – Manjula Sethi

MANJULA SETHI

Manjula Sethi was born in Rawalpindi on 20th September 1944 and did her schooling in Rampur and college in Bhopal. Manjula was an educationist and retired as the Head Mistress of BHEL Education Department, Bhopal.

Manjula married Surinder Pal Kumar on 10th October 1961. Surinder Pal Kumar was born on 12th June 1936 in Gujranwala, now in Pakistan. Surinder Pal worked with BHEL, Bhopal and retired from BHEL as Dy. General Manager, Technical Services Department.

Manjula and Late Surinder Pal Kumar have two sons, Rajeev Kumar (born on 17th March 1963) and Sanjeev Kumar (born on 13th November 1964). Manjula presently lives in Bhopal along with her family.

Kulwant Rai Sethi – Harjas Rai Sethi – Sukhanand Sethi – Ram Krishan Sethi – Dani Ditta Lal Sethi – Narsingh Das Sethi – Ganesh Das Sethi – Chaman Lal Sethi – Reena Sethi

REENA SETHI

Reena Sethi was born on 6th December 1946 at Rawalpindi. She completed her schooling and college from Rampur and after graduation got married to Jatinder Kalia in Ambala. Jatinder started his career with BHEL in Bhopal as an Engineer after which they shifted to USA.

Reena and Jatinder live in USA. Reena is a property broker in Pittsburgh and Jatinder retired as a Thermal Pipeline Engineer.

Kulwant Rai Sethi – Harjas Rai Sethi – Sukhanand Sethi – Ram Krishan Sethi – Dani Ditta Lal Sethi – Narsingh Das Sethi – Ganesh Das Sethi – Chaman Lal Sethi – Meenakshi Sethi

MEENAKSHI SETHI

Meenakshi Sethi was born on 20th December 1948 at Rampur. She completed her studies from Moradabad and got married to Krishna Kapoor who was born and brought up in Bombay. After marriage Meenakshi and Krishna moved to Kuwait where they worked with Air India. They later shifted to Maryland in USA, and worked with American Express, Maryland. Krishna died in 2019. Meenakshi presently lives in USA. Meenakshi and Krishan hace two children Anjana and Amit.

Kulwant Rai Sethi – Harjas Rai Sethi – Sukhanand Sethi – Ram Krishan Sethi – Dani Ditta Lal Sethi – Narsingh Das Sethi – Ganesh Das Sethi – Chaman Lal Sethi – Arun Sethi

ARUN SETHI

Arun Sethi, the youngest son of Chaman Lal Sethi and Satya was born on 10th October 1949 at Rampur. He completed his studies from Moradabad and moved to Kuwait where he worked with the Department of Electricity and Water Supply.

Arun married Neelima Sharma on 12th October 1976 at Moradabad. Neelima was from Moradabad and was born on 7th October 1956. When the political situation in Kuwait worsened due to the unrest Arun and Neelima returned to India and settled in Moradabad where he started a unit manufacturing Corrugated box.

Arun and Neelima are settled in Moradabad and have a son, Ashu Sethi and two daughters Priya Sethi and Preeti Sethi.

Kulwant Rai Sethi – Harjas Rai Sethi – Sukhanand Sethi – Ram Krishan Sethi – Dani Ditta Lal Sethi – Narsingh Das Sethi – Ganesh Das Sethi – Kaushalya Sethi

KAUSHALYA SETHI (SABHARWAL) and FAMILY

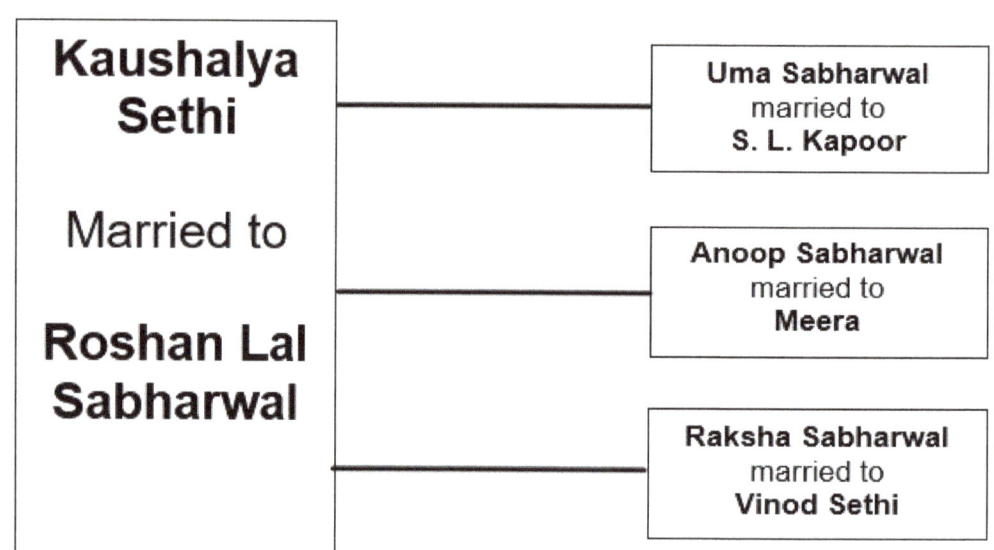

Kulwant Rai Sethi – Harjas Rai Sethi – Sukhanand Sethi – Ram Krishan Sethi – Dani Ditta Lal Sethi – Narsingh Das Sethi – Ganesh Das Sethi – Kaushalya Sethi – Uma Sabharwal

UMA SABHARWAL

Uma Sabharwal was born in Rawalpindi on 8th January 1942. She got married to Mr. S.L. Kapur who used to work in a government office. Uma and S.L. Kapur had two sons, Ajay and Atul.

Kulwant Rai Sethi – Harjas Rai Sethi – Sukhanand Sethi – Ram Krishan Sethi – Dani Ditta Lal Sethi – Narsingh Das Sethi – Ganesh Das Sethi – Kaushalya Sethi – Anoop Sabharwal

ANOOP SABHARWAL

Anoop Sabharwal was born on December 20, 1937, in Lahore. He spent his early years studying in Karachi and across India before joining Sir JJ College of Art in Bombay. However, after a few months, he secured admission to the National Defence Academy (NDA) at the age of 17. Upon completing his course at NDA he joined the Indian Navy, where he served across coastal India, primarily in Bombay and Visakhapatnam.

In the late 1960s, Anoop commanded INS Magar and was briefly posted on INS Khukri, which was tragically sunk by a Pakistani submarine during the 1971 war. During the war, he was actively involved in harbour defence and the recovery of parts from PNS Ghazi, the Pakistani submarine destroyed by the Indian Navy. Later, he commanded the missile boat INS Veer.

Towards the end of his naval career, he was posted at Naval Headquarters in Delhi. After 20 years of commissioned service in 1980 Anoop Sabharwal took premature retirement as a Lieutenant Commander and transitioned to the Merchant Navy, serving as a ship captain until 1993.

On June 12, 1966, Anoop Sabharwal married Meera Sabharwal in Ambala. Meera was born on March 18, 1946, in Gujarat, Undivided India. In the 1980s, while raising their two sons, Aman Sabharwal and Amit Sabharwal, she pursued a degree in law and became a practicing lawyer in Dehradun.

Kulwant Rai Sethi – Harjas Rai Sethi – Sukhanand Sethi – Ram Krishan Sethi – Dani Ditta Lal Sethi – Narsingh Das Sethi – Ganesh Das Sethi – Kaushalya Sethi – Raksha Sabharwal

RAKSHA SABHARWAL

Raksha Sabharwal was born on 12th September 1947 at Karachi. She had her schooling in Modi Nagar and did her college in Ambala and Saharanpur.

After graduation Raksha started working for Plastichemicals Pvt. Limited in Delhi (a Company owned by her cousin, Satish Anand).

Raksha Sabharwal got married to Vinod Sethi on 1st October 1979 at Delhi. Vinod Sethi was born on 9th November 1946 at Lahore. He specialised in Excise matters and worked for Flex Industries and Hero Honda.

Raksha and Vinod Sethi live in Faridabad and have a daughter, Smriti (born on 16th October 1980).

Kulwant Rai Sethi – Harjas Rai Sethi – Sukhanand Sethi – Ram Krishan Sethi – Dani Ditta Lal Sethi – Narsingh Das Sethi – Ganesh Das Sethi – Raj Dulari Sethi

7) RAJ DULARI SETHI (BHASIN) and FAMILY

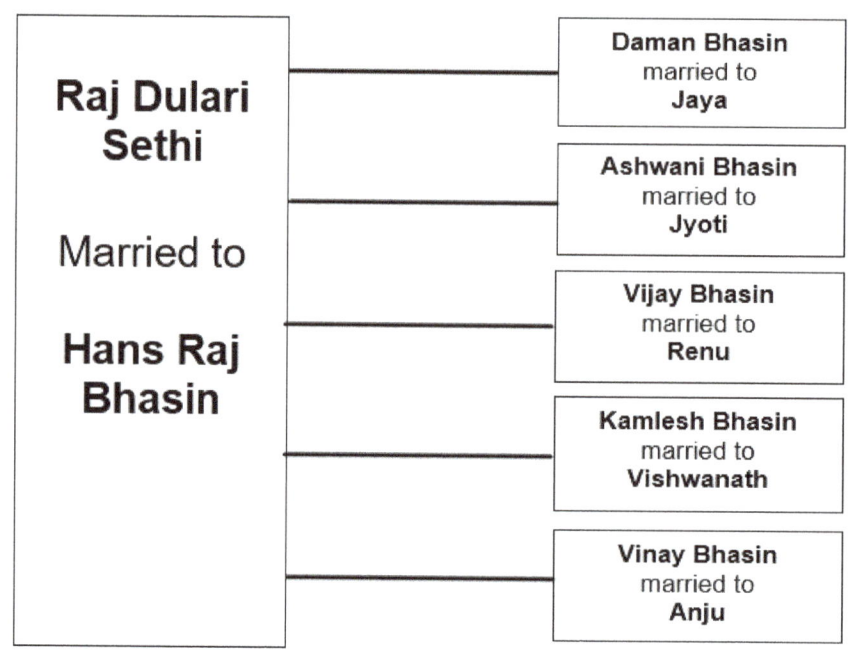

Kulwant Rai Sethi – Harjas Rai Sethi – Sukhanand Sethi – Ram Krishan Sethi – Dani Ditta Lal Sethi – Narsingh Das Sethi – Ganesh Das Sethi – Raj Dulari Sethi – Daman Bhasin

DAMAN BHASIN

Daman Bhasin was born on 28th December 1936 at Rawalpindi. He studied in Rawalpindi and Ambala and later joined Oil and Natural Gas Commission. Daman Bhasin specialised in controlling offshore oil well fires and was the General Manager – Drilling with ONGC when he retired. His specialization in this field took him to several countries to advise and train the oil well fires and oil drilling personnel there.

During his tenure with ONGC in Ahmedabad and Mehsana, Daman Bhasin met Jayashree Patel (Jaya) who hailed from Mehsana. Jaya was born on 22nd September 1951. They fell in love and decided to get married. However, Jaya's parents were against the match due to the difference in age, family backgrounds and caste etc. Despite their resistance the couple took a call and got married in Ambala on 6th March 1971 with the blessings of Daman's parents and elders of the family.

Having been posted in various parts of the country, including Gujarat, Assam and Dehradun, Daman and Jaya decided to settle in Dehradun after Daman's retirement from ONGC. They continue to live in Dehradun and have two daughters, Seema (born in 1972), Veena (born in 1976) and a son Gagan (born in 1978).

Kulwant Rai Sethi – Harjas Rai Sethi – Sukhanand Sethi – Ram Krishan Sethi – Dani Ditta Lal Sethi – Narsingh Das Sethi – Ganesh Das Sethi – Raj Dulari Sethi – Ashwani Bhasin

ASHWANI BHASIN

Ashwani Bhasin, fondly called as Kumar was born on 5th November 1940 at Lahore. Ashwani studied at D.A.V. College in Ambala and later graduated from Bhartiya Vidyapeeth, Poona.

He started his career as a central Government Employee and got married to Jyoti Mukul on 25th June 1983. Jyoti was born on 17th September 1953 at Ahmedabad and had studied at Diwan Ballubhai School, Ahmedabad.

Ashwani and Jyoti have two sons, Rajiv (born on 11th June 1984), Sanjeev (born on 31st May 1986) and a daughter Shelika (born on 23rd October 1991. Ashwani left for his heavenly abode on 22nd January 2011. Jyoti lives in Gurugram (Gurgaon) with her children.

Kulwant Rai Sethi – Harjas Rai Sethi – Sukhanand Sethi – Ram Krishan Sethi – Dani Ditta Lal Sethi – Narsingh Das Sethi – Ganesh Das Sethi – Raj Dulari Sethi – Vijay Bhasin

VIJAY BHASIN

Vijay Bhasin was born on 24th February 1942 at Rawalpindi. He studied in Ambala and later joined the family Timber business.

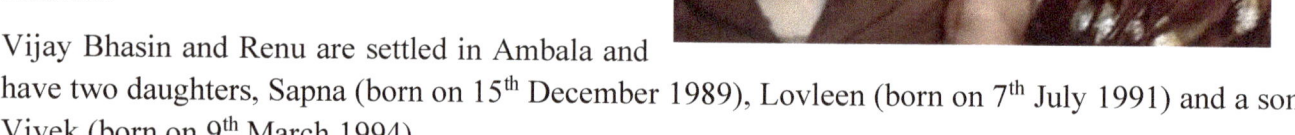

Vijay Bhasin got married on 23rd September 1988 in Chandigarh to Renu who was born on 28th October 1954. Renu is a retired Government Employee who worked with the Forest Research Institute.

Vijay Bhasin and Renu are settled in Ambala and have two daughters, Sapna (born on 15th December 1989), Lovleen (born on 7th July 1991) and a son Vivek (born on 9th March 1994).

Kulwant Rai Sethi – Harjas Rai Sethi – Sukhanand Sethi – Ram Krishan Sethi – Dani Ditta Lal Sethi – Narsingh Das Sethi – Ganesh Das Sethi – Raj Dulari Sethi – Kamlesh Bhasin

KAMLESH BHASIN

Kamlesh Bhasin was born on 8th September 1944 at Lahore. After the partition her parents migrated to Ambala from where Kamlesh completed school and college.

Kamlesh Bhasin went on to become a Gazetted Officer.

Kamlesh got married at Delhi on 4th March 1972 to Vishwanath, who was a businessman and had business interests in Delhi. Kamlesh and Vishwanath have a daughter, Vandana (born on 30th December 1975).

Kulwant Rai Sethi – Harjas Rai Sethi – Sukhanand Sethi – Ram Krishan Sethi – Dani Ditta Lal Sethi – Narsingh Das Sethi – Ganesh Das Sethi – Raj Dulari Sethi – Vinay Bhasin

VINAY BHASIN

Vinay Bhasin was the youngest in the family and was born on 22nd December 1945 at Rawalpindi.

Vinay had his schooling in Ambala and went on to join the family Timber business. Thet were the largest timber merchants of Ambala.

Vinay Bhasin got married to Anju on 24th July 2000 at Ambala Cantt.

Anju was born on 16th October 1969 and completed her studies from Kurukshetra University. Vinay Bhasin and Anju have a son, Ansh (born on 24th December 2005).

Kulwant Rai Sethi – Harjas Rai Sethi – Sukhanand Sethi – Ram Krishan Sethi – Dani Ditta Lal Sethi – Narsingh Das Sethi – Ganesh Das Sethi – Narendra Nath Sethi

8) NARENDRA NATH SETHI and FAMILY

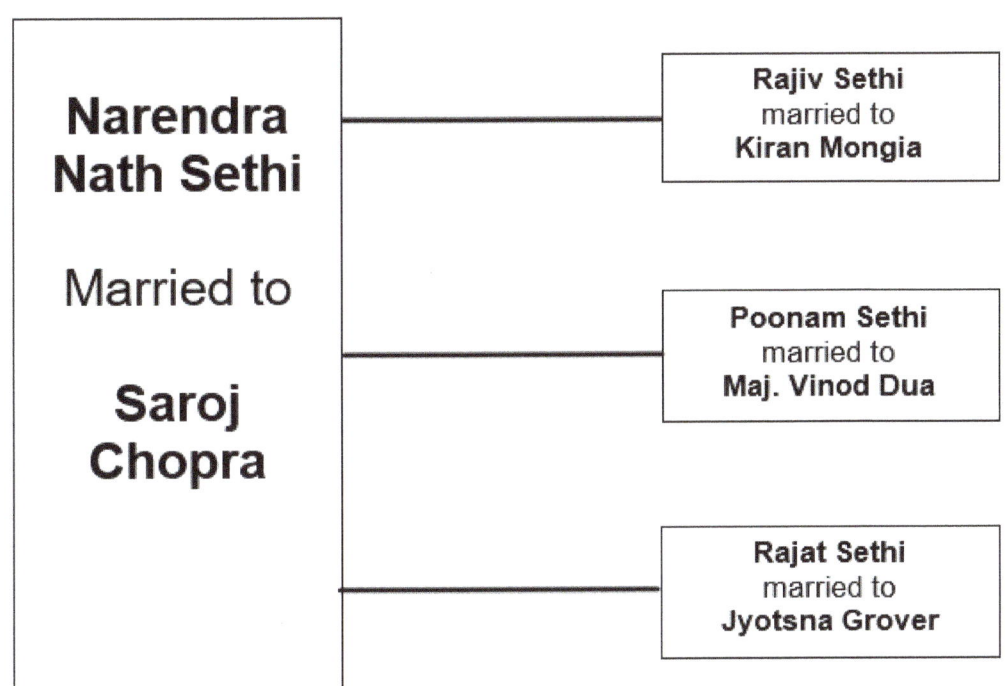

Kulwant Rai Sethi – Harjas Rai Sethi – Sukhanand Sethi – Ram Krishan Sethi – Dani Ditta Lal Sethi – Narsingh Das Sethi – Ganesh Das Sethi – Narendra Nath Sethi – Rajiv Sethi

RAJIV SETHI

Rajiv Sethi was born on February 6, 1953, in Kanpur. He was in Class 6 at Methodist High School when he lost his father, Narendra Nath Sethi. Shortly after, he was admitted to Birla Public School, a boarding school in Pilani, where he completed his higher secondary education.

A passionate mountaineer, Rajiv found solace in the Himalayas, trekking extensively and achieving the remarkable feat of scaling the 18,000 ft Har Bhagwan peak at just 16 years old.

Upon returning to Kanpur, he aspired to become a doctor, but financial constraints forced him to reconsider. Instead, he pursued a Bachelor of Commerce (B.Com.) degree from Kanpur University, where he excelled and earned a place on the university's merit list. His achievement earned him a scholarship, but the trauma of the early loss of his father and witnessing his mother's struggles had left a lasting impact on him. Determined to support her, Rajiv chose to enter the workforce early, prioritizing his family's well-being over further studies.

Rajiv Sethi's professional journey began in Calcutta, where he joined Business Forms Limited. Recognized for his dedication and skills, he was promoted within two years as the Branch Manager in Ahmedabad.

Over the next 14 years, he rose through the ranks, working in Bombay and Kanpur as Regional Manager, before returning to Calcutta as Marketing Head. Eventually, Rajiv moved back to Kanpur and started his own business. After 14 years in business, Rajiv decided to shift to Ahmedabad and joined Ginni International Limited a textile company based at Neemrana as their marketing head at Ahmedabad. He retired n 2020.

Beyond his career, Rajiv has been deeply committed to social service, especially through Freemasonry.

His contributions include establishing India's first Computerized Braille Language Centre, a Computer Centre for Hearing and Speech Impaired individuals in Ahmedabad, and a Centre for Paraplegics in Bhuj, among other impactful initiatives. Giving back to society remains his enduring passion.

In 1976, Rajiv Sethi met Kiran Mongia in Ahmedabad and they got married on May 19, 1977 at Kanpur.

Kiran Mongia is the daughter of Mr. Madan Lal Mongia and Prakash Mongia (both deceased) with their roots from the Multan (now in Pakistan).

Kiran, born on February 11, 1957, completed her schooling in Kanpur before earning a Diploma in Hotel Management from Sophia College, Bombay. Kiran Mongia later pursued a postgraduate degree in English and Special English.

Over the years, she has taught English and Social Studies. She served as Principal and Academic Director of a school in Ahmedabad.

Kiran Mongia Sethi worked as a freelancer with various BPOs at Ahmedabad.

Currently, Kiran is a freelancer with IDP Australia based in Ahmedabad. She is also on the Board of Directors of ITOWE, an NGO doing commendable work in educational reforms throughout the country.

With a creative spirit, Kiran finds joy in writing, painting, music, and storytelling. Theatre is her first love, and she has acted in and directed numerous Hindi plays, both amateur and professional. Her plays were also telecast through Doordarshan.

Kiran's poetry collection, *"I Believe"* was recently published and was nominated for the prestigious "Emmy Dickenson Award."

Rajiv shares a passion for adventure sports, particularly mountaineering trekking, horse riding, skydiving, paragliding, para scootering, zip line, scuba diving, dune driving, among other thrilling pursuits.

Rajiv Sethi and Kiran Mongia Sethi are settled in Ahmedabad.

Rajiv and Kiran's children, Anubhav Sethi (born August 24, 1979) and Aanchal Sethi (born February 24, 1982), have built their lives in Dubai and Singapore, respectively.

Rajiv and Kiran with their family – Anubhav Namita, Nitesh, Aanchal and Reyankh

Kulwant Rai Sethi – Harjas Rai Sethi – Sukhanand Sethi – Ram Krishan Sethi – Dani Ditta Lal Sethi – Narsingh Das Sethi – Ganesh Das Sethi – Narendra Nath Sethi – Poonam Sethi

POONAM SETHI

Poonam Sethi was born on 26th August 1954 in Lucknow. Shortly after her 9th birthday on 1st September 1963, she lost her father to a sudden heart attack. Her courageous mother, Saroj Sethi, began working at BIC within a month to support the family.

Poonam studied at Methodist High School, Kanpur, before joining Birla Balika Vidyapeeth, Pilani, in March 1964, as a Class 6 student. She actively participated in extracurricular activities and excelled in several. She was the school swimming champion, hockey captain, and particularly stood out in drama, debates, and elocution. She was also a part of the famous Pilani Band and had the honor of participating in the Republic Day Parade in Delhi twice.

Her passion for theatre continued even after marriage. She took part in Sangeet Natak Academy competitions and performed at Prithvi Theatre, Bombay.

Poonam completed her graduation from Christ Church College, Kanpur, and later pursued a Postgraduate course in Tourism and Travel from Sophia Polytechnic, Bombay. She worked briefly with Air India, Bombay, before joining Sita World Travel, Kanpur, as an Assistant Manager for two years. Later, she turned entrepreneur and founded Granny's Touch, a small enterprise specializing in infant garments, supplying to stores like Mothercare across India. She later expanded her brand to include clothing for children up to 12 years, renaming it Baby Talk.

Beyond business, Poonam has been actively involved in social work, collaborating with an NGO in Delhi focused on women and childcare.

Since 2008, she has been running Indicraft, an enterprise that works with artisans to create handcrafted home décor products, supplying them to hotels and individuals.

On 4th September 1976, Poonam married Captain Vinod Dua, an infantry officer from the National Defence Academy, serving with the Jammu and Kashmir Rifles.

Vinod Dua was born on 3rd August 1947 in Moradabad to Mr. Manohar Lal Dua and Mrs. Janak (Sethi) Dua. He studied at Methodist High School, Kanpur prior to Joining the National Defence Academy.

Poonam and Vinod Dua were blessed with two children, daughter Upasana, born on 19th September 1977, and son Anuj, born on 11th February 1980.

Sadly, Vinod passed away in March 2008.

Poonam currently resides in Noida.

Kulwant Rai Sethi – Harjas Rai Sethi – Sukhanand Sethi – Ram Krishan Sethi – Dani Ditta Lal Sethi – Narsingh Das Sethi – Ganesh Das Sethi – Narendra Nath Sethi – Rajat Sethi

RAJAT SETHI

Rajat Sethi born on 28th February 1958 in Meerut is enjoying a retired life after hanging up his boots from corporate life. Rajat did his Advanced Management Program from Harvard Business School after completing his MBA from University Business School, Chandigarh, graduation in BA (Honours) in Economics from Sriram College of Commerce, Delhi University and schooling from Methodist High School, Kanpur.

In his earlier avatar, Rajat headed several global marketing communication companies such as Lintas, McCann Erickson, Wunderman, Dentsu and Reader's Digest.

Rajat has also been a jury member at the Cannes Advertising Festival as well as the International Echo awards. He was voted as the Asia Pacific Agency Head of the Year by Campaign magazine, Hongkong and he has also been presented with the McCann Leadership Award.

Post retirement, Rajat is pursuing his passion for Photography, Golf, Tennis, Birding and traveling. He is also an advanced certified Scuba diver.

Rajat got married to Jyotsna Grover on 14th April 1986 at Kanpur. Jyotsna was born in Nagpur on 8th December1964. Her father Sq. Ldr. Ravindra Lal Grover passed away in service at a very young age. Her mother, Shashi Grover, brought up Jyotsna and her brother, as an entrepreneur running a cooking gas agency in Kanpur.

Jyotsna has been a senior Immigration Officer in the High Commission of Canada since the past two decades. She did her schooling from Maharani Gayatri Devi (MGD) school in Jaipur and her graduation from Jesus and Mary College, Delhi University.

Jyotsna is passionate about promoting the dying art of Handloom Saree weaving and wearing and has travelled across India visiting weavers in villages and understanding their plight and the challenges they face.

Rajat and Jyotsna live in Noida and have two daughters, Devika (born on 21st April 1987) and Nandini (born on 28th May 1990) who live in Singapore and Hongkong respectively.

Rajat and Jyotsna with their family – Devika Ayesha, Varun Nandini, Anubhav and Vivaan

TENTH, ELEVENTH, TWELFTH AND THIRTEENTH GENERATIONS

Kulwant Rai Sethi – Harjas Rai Sethi – Sukhanand Sethi – Ram Krishan Sethi – Dani Ditta Lal Sethi – Narsingh Das Sethi – Ganesh Das Sethi – Amolak Ram Sethi - Pushpa Sethi (Behl)

PUSHPA SETHI (BEHL) and FAMILY

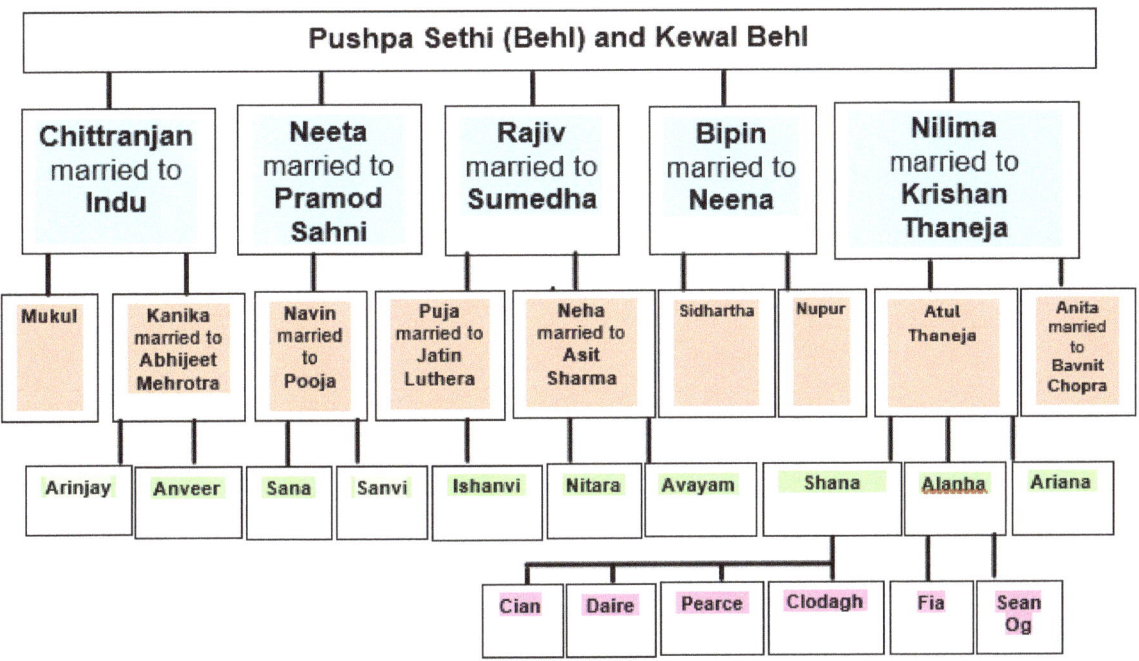

Pushpa Sethi (Behl) and Kewal Behl had five children, Chittranjan Behl Nilima Behl, Rajiv Behl, Bipin Behl and Neeta Behl.

Nilima Behl was born during the pre-partition era on 22nd November 1946 at Lahore. After the partition her parent's shifted to Lucknow where Nilima studied at Loretto Convent and Isabella Thorburn College from where she studied English Lit. Psychology, World history and Political Science. After her marriage to Krishan Thaneja, Nilima and Krishan moved to UK in 1968.

In UK Nilima worked with the post office and later as Peoples Manager with British Airways which was her last job prior to retirement. Nilima practices Nicherin Buddhism and is fond of travelling and cooking.

Nilima got married to Krishan Thaneja on 22nd February 1968 at New Delhi. Krishan Thaneja was born on 18th October 1841 at Nairobi and since 1968 was settled in UK. He had specialised in Accountancy and worked with RCA Record's and Mark Allen Travel. A keen traveller and Badminton player he sadly left for his heavenly abode on 17th March 2023. Nilima and Krishan have a daughter, Anita Thaneja and a son Atul Thaneja. Nilima and Krishan are proud great grandparents to 6 great grandchildren of the only thirteenth generation.

Anita Thaneja was born on 27th April 1969 in London. She did her postgraduate in Languages and Business and works as a Customer Service Provider with American Airlines. Anita is a fitness freak and loves to travel and learn different languages Anita got married in London on 26th March 2016 to Bavnit Chopra who was born in London on 9th September 1970. Bavnit completed his Aviation from UK and is the Regional Manager with American Airlines. A keen traveller he is also fond of Cricket, Football and Cooking.

Atul Thaneja was born on 1st October 1971 at London. He completed his business studies and is an entrepreneur running his own business in London. Atul is a keen football player and interested in travelling cooking and DIY. Atul is divorced and **has** three daughters, Shana, Alanah and Ariana.

Shana has three sons, **Cian**, **Daire** and **Pearce** and a daughter **Clodagh**. **Alanah** has a son, **Sean Og** and a daughter, **Fia**. **Ariana** is currently studying Finance at a University in London.

Neelima with her great grandchildren – the 13th Generation

Chittranjan Behl, the eldest of this family's tenth generation was born in Lahore on 10th September 1944. He did his initial schooling in Lucknow and thereafter completed his Hotel Management from Pusa Institute Delhi. Chittranjan then went to Germany and Canada for training. He started his career in the hospitality sector with Clarks Avadh in Lucknow and later joined Taj Hotels. During his tenure with Taj Hotels he was posted at Bombay, Goa and Chennai.

Chittaranjan later joined Centaur Hotel Bombay as Director Operations. His journey in hospitality took him to Holiday Inn Bangalore as their General Manager. At the last leg of his career Chittranjan joined Sun N Sand, Pune and retired from there in 2013 as their Chief General Manager.

Chittranjan Behl got married to Indu on 29th September 1974 at Delhi. Indu was born on 7th February 1953 at Ludhiana and graduated from Institute of Home Economics Delhi. Chittranjan and Indu have two children Mukul and Kanika. Chittranjan and Indu are now settled in Pune.

Mukul was born on 30th October 1976 in Delhi and lives with his parents in Pune.

Kanika was born on 6th May 1979 at Bombay and graduated in Human Resources from Delhi after which she did her Post Graduation from Symbiosis, Pune, specialising in Human Resources. She worked in Singapore and Ireland as HR Manager with Google. Kanika got married on 27th November 2005 to Abhijeet Mehrotra who was born on 18th October 1978 at Agra. Abhijeet is an IIT Kanpur graduate and worked with Coca Cola in Singapore and presently is the Director IT Wing at Coca Cola in Atlanta. **Kanika** and Abhijeet have two children, Arinjay (born on 12th September 2008) and Anveer (born on 18th July 2016). **Arinjay** is studying in the 12th Std. and preparing for CAT/SAT. **Ariveer** is presently in the 3rd Std. The family is settled in Atlanta USA.

Rajiv Behl, was born in Lucknow on 10th May 1948 and studied in Boys School Lucknow.

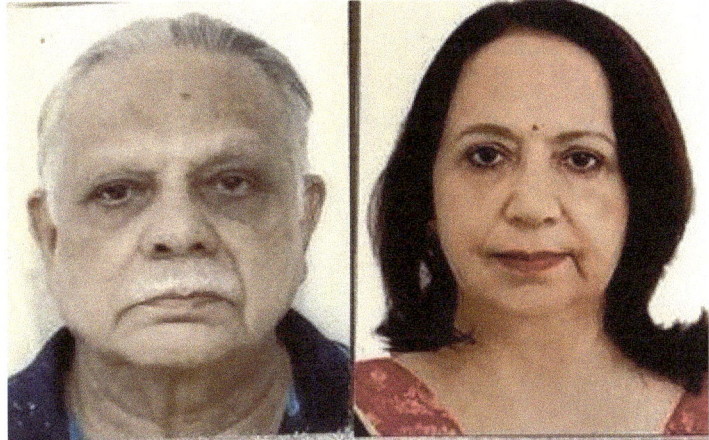

He completed his post-graduation in MA/LLB from Delhi University after which Rajiv Behl worked with National Textile Corporation, New Delhi and retired from there in 2007 as their General Manager.

Rajiv Behl got married to Sumedha on 20th May 1978 at Delhi. Sumedha was born on 27th August 1957 at Ambala Cantt. She completed her graduation with BA from Lady Shriram College and thereafter worked with National Building

Construction Corporation and retired as their Dy. General Manager in 2017. Rajiv and Sumedha have two daughters, Pooja Behl and Neha Behl.

Pooja Behl was born on 7th June 1979 at Delhi. She completed her MBA from Shriram College of Commerce, Delhi University. She is presently CHRO with Trident group of Companies. Poojal Behl got married to Jatin Luthra who is a co-founder of Jet Life, a startup in Educational Tools. Pooja and Jatin have a daughter **Ishaanvi** who was born on 9th May 2009 and presently is in Class 11.

Neha Behl was born on 18th September 1984 at Delhi. She completed her MBA from Xavier Institute of Management, Bhubaneshwar and worked in PWC. Neha Behl is married to Asit Sharma who is working in South Korea. Neha and Asit have a daughter, **Nitara** who was born on 22nd June 2017 and a son **Avyam** born on 22nd June 2021.

Bipin Krishan Behl, was born in Lucknow on 20th August 1950. His initial education took place in St. Francis, Lucknow and he continued his school education in Delhi after his family shifted there. He graduated in 1974 from Delhi University after which he joined National Tobacco Co. as a sales trainee and thereafter in 1979 joined Golden Tobacco Co. as Field Manager. In 1984 Bipin moved to Birla's Orient Fans and retired from there on 31st December 2008 as the Regional Manager (North). After retirement he has been handling logistics of products of Orient Fans in Haryana.

Bipin Behl got married to Neena on 22nd October 1980 at Delhi. Neena was born in Delhi on 31st July 1955. She completed her school education in Punjab and graduated with MSc. from Punjab University. Bipin and Neena have a daughter, Nupur Behl and a son Sidhartha Behl.

Nupur Behl was born on 10th February 1984 in Delhi. She studied at Delhi Public School and graduated with a Masters in English Honors from Delhi University. After doing a teaching course from Delhi University she joined Genesis School, Noida as an English Teacher.

Sidhartha Behl was born on 2nd March 1988 in Delhi. He did his schooling in Delhi and graduated from Amity Noida in Journalism. He also joined Jamia in Delhi and specialised in photography.

Sidhartha worked with Seeds NGO for disaster management and later became a freelance photographer. He has a contract with National Geographic Channel and is in USA for the presentation of his work. His photographs have been published in leading magazines.

Neeta Behl, was born in Lucknow on 4th September 1952. She did her schooling at La Martiner, Lucknow and graduated from Delhi University. Neeta is an avid reader.

Neeta Behl got married to Pramod Sahni on 9th December 1973 at Delhi. Pramod was born in Rawalpindi on 13th July 1945.

Pramod Sahni studied in DAV College and later joined the National Defence Academy and was commissioned in the Indian army.

Pramod Sahni retired as a Brigadier. He was a keen horse rider, golfer and a great swimmer. Being in the Army,

Pramod and Neeta were posted at various places. Brig. Pramod left for his heavenly abode in 1992. Neeta presently lives in Mumbai.

Neeta and Pramod have a son, Navin Sahni.

Navin Sahni was born on 3rd March 1975 in Dehradun. He studied at Army Public School, Delhi and graduated from Pusa Institute Delhi, in Hotel Management.

Navin Sahni presently is the Senior Vice President at Reliance Nippon, Mumbai. He is a keen foodie and fond of cars and travelling.

Navin Sahni got married to Pooja on 4th November 2003 at Delhi.

Pooja was born on 23rd June 1976 in Lucknow. She studied at St. Joseph Convent and Kendriya Vidyalaya and later graduated from DAV College. Pooja is an educationist.

Navin and Pooja have two daughters **Sana Sahni** and **Sanvi Sahni** and are settled in Mumbai.

Sana Sahni was born on 8th December 2005 at Noida. She studied at Amity International School and is doing her graduation from Mithibai College of Arts, Mumbai. She is a keen artist, and a graphic designer interested in Social Media marketing.

Sanvi Sahni was born on 15th November 2007 in Gurgaon and is studying in Army International School. She is a keen horse rider interested in Animal Welfare and fond of baking and cooking.

Kulwant Rai Sethi – Harjas Rai Sethi – Sukhanand Sethi – Ram Krishan Sethi – Dani Ditta Lal Sethi – Narsingh Das Sethi – Ganesh Das Sethi – Amolak Ram Sethi – Tilak Raj Sethi

TILAK RAJ SETHI and FAMILY

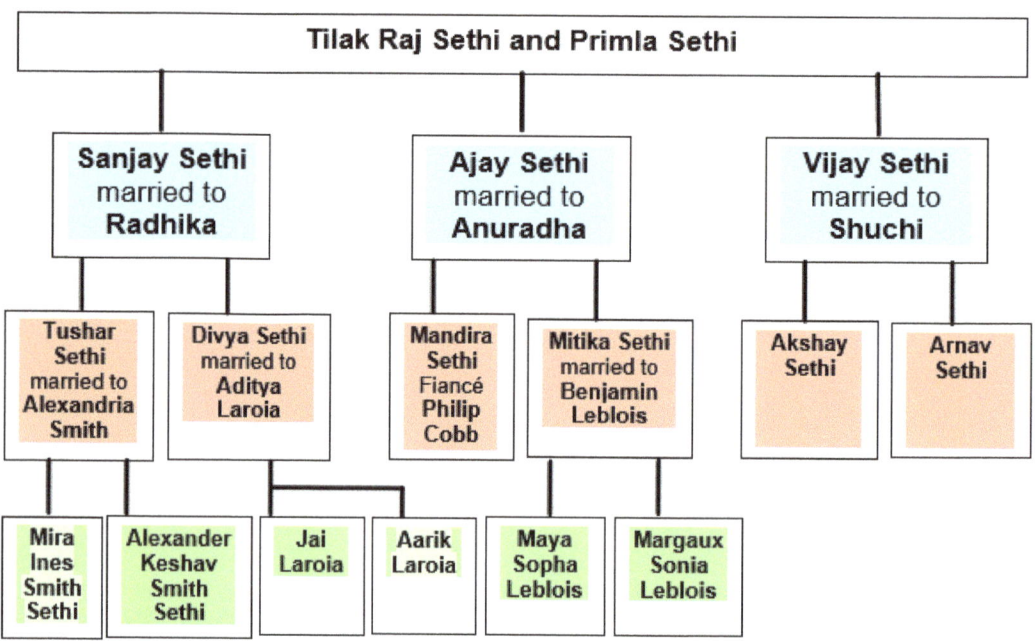

Tilak Raj Sethi and Primla had three children, Sanjay Sethi, Ajay Sethi and Vijay Sethi.

Sanjay Sethi, the eldest of this families tenth generation was born in Srinagar on 16th August 1951. Sanjay's initial schooling was at Burnhall, Srinagar after which he went to Mayo College Ajmer and later graduated from St. Xaviers College Calcutta. After graduation Sanjay went to London and completed Accountancy from Touche Ross.

After returning from London, Sanjay settled in Delhi and started his own consultancy firm pertaining to the shipping industry and represented three overseas companies and was a consultant to many other companies in India and overseas.

On 12th August 1978, Sanjay got married to Radhika Rattan who was born on 31st March 1951 in Simla.

Radhika did her schooling in Bombay in St. Annes, St. Joseph's Presentation Convent, Srinagar and Atabai Petit's School. Radhika graduated in Sociology from Sophia College, Bombay.

Sanjay Sethi and Radhika have two children, **Tushar Sethi** and **Diya Sethi.**

Tushar Sethi was born on 27th August 1981 in Delhi. He studied in Tiny Tots Delhi and then moved to Mayo College, Ajmer. Tushar did his under graduation from Emory University, Atlanta and master's from London School of Economics. Tushar Sethi moved to the USA for a few years and worked with Merrill Lyeth handling Diverse Securities Investment Banking. From the USA he moved to London and did his masters in Environment Technology from Imperial College. He specialized in Environmental and Geospatial Technologies and started his own company "Margosa Environmental Solutions" based in London.

Tushar married Alexandria on 29th March 2016. Alexandria was born on 14th November 1982. She also did her undergrad from Emory University after which she did a double PhD in Mental Health and Epidemiology.

Tushar Sethi and Alexandria Smith have a daughter **Mira Ines Smith Sethi** (born on 6th July 2018) and a son **Alexander Keshav Smith Sethi** (born on 28th November 2021).

Diya Sethi was born on 23rd October 1984 in Delhi. She studied at Airforce Bal Bharti School Delhi and Sriram School Delhi.

Diya Sethi later went to London for further studies and did Graphic design from London College of Communication (University of Arts, London). Diya returned to Delhi and started her own business in Graphic Designing.

Diya married Aditya Laroia on 27th November 2016 in Delhi. Aditya is from Delhi and studied at St. Columbus, Delhi. He later did his undergrad and graduation from the USA. Aditya worked for Lehman Bros. and thereafter as the head of sales Asia Pacific at Saxo Markets and Head of wholesale Trading and financing, EMEA at Nomura. In 2020 Aditya joined Maybank and on 18th May 2021 was appointed 'Chief Executive Officer of Maybank Securities Pte. Ltd.

Settled in Singapore, Diya and Aditya have two sons, **Jai Laroia** (born on 10th July 2019) and **Aarik Laroia** (born on 9th April 2022).

Ajay Sethi was born in Guwahati on 4th June 1957. His initial schooling was in Calcutta and thereafter he studied at Mayo College Ajmer. After completing his bachelor's degree Ajay Sethi joined the In-house Hotel Management course of ITC Limited and joined the ITC Hotel at Agra after the completion of the course.

Ajay Sethi married Anu on 18th June 1983. Anu was born on 17th August 1962 and after completing her bachelor's degree she did hotel management at IHM Pusa Road, Delhi. She met Ajay when she joined ITC Hotels after the completion of the course. After their respective stints with ITC Hotels Ajay and Anu moved to the United States and worked in the hotel industry there.

Ajay Sethi and Anu Sethi have two daughters Mandira and Mitika. Ajay Sethi died on 16th January 2013. Anu Sethi lives in the USA and is a business owner.

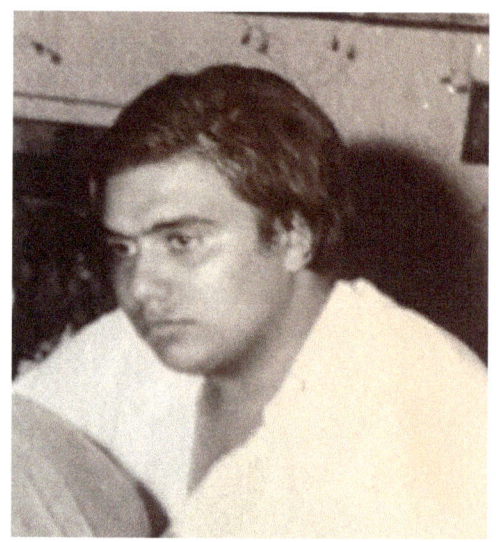

Mandira Sethi was born on 26th December 1985 in Delhi. She completed her graduation and settled in the USA.

Mandira is a Juris Doctor of Counsel at Barnes and Thornburg. Her fiancé Philip Cobb was born on 23rd August 1990. He is an MBA, working as a Sr. Financial Analyst at 'Interface', USA.

Mitika Sethi was born in Delhi on 19th June 1989. She settled in the US after completing graduation. Mitika is presently The Director of Examinations at the Federal Reserve Bank of Atlanta.

Mitika married Benjamin (Ben) Leblois on 24th November 2018 in the USA. Benjamin was born on 23rd August 1989 and after completing his bachelors and MBA he started "Bricks for Kids" and is a global investor focusing on companies in Africa and Central Eastern Europe.

Mitika and Benjamin have two daughters, **Maya Sophia Leblois** (born on 23rd October 2020) and **Margaux Sonia Leblois** (born on 4th August 2023).

Vijay Sethi, the youngest of this families tenth generation was born in Delhi on 2nd November 1963. Vijay studied in Don Bosco School in Calcutta (Kolkata) till, his father, Tilak Raj Sethi retired and shifted to Delhi. Thereafter he studied at APJ Malviya Nagar, New Delhi. Vijay completed his graduation from Bhagat Singh College, Delhi University. He was a keen Sportsman and played Cricket and Table Tennis and represented his School and College.

Vijay Sethi worked with Bata India for a year and then started his own business in 1985.

Vijay Sethi married Shuchi Chandhok on 16th February 1991.

Shuchi was born in Delhi on 12th November 1967 and had her schooling at Presentation Convent, Srinagar and graduated from Women's College Srinagar. Shuchi initially worked as a Kindergarten Teacher and is now a home maker and an excellent cook. Her cooking skills are highly appreciated. Both Vijay and Shuchi are fond of travelling, gardening and outdoor activities.

Vijay Sethi and Shuchi have two sons, **Akshay Sethi** and **Arnav Sethi**.

Akshay Sethi was born in May 1994 in Delhi. He completed his schooling at Amity International Noida and graduated from Sri Venkateswara College, Delhi University.

He is a keen traveler and a qualified diver. Akshay Sethi worked with 'Zomato' in India and then joined 'Talabat' in the UAE and was there for five years. He is now pursuing his MBA from INSEAD.

Arnav Sethi was born in Delhi in September 1996. He did his schooling from Step by Step, Noida and graduation from Hindu College, Delhi University.

Arnav Sethi pursued his studies further and did his MA and MPhil from JNU and Delhi School of Economics.

Presently Arnav Sethi is doing his PhD from the University of Cambridge as a Cambridge Trust Scholar. Arnav Sethi is a trained Indian Classical Musician and has participated in many music concerts.

Kulwant Rai Sethi – Harjas Rai Sethi – Sukhanand Sethi – Ram Krishan Sethi – Dani Ditta Lal Sethi – Narsingh Das Sethi – Ganesh Das Sethi – Amolak Ram Sethi – Kanchan Sethi (Madan)

KANCHAN SETHI (MADAN) and FAMILY

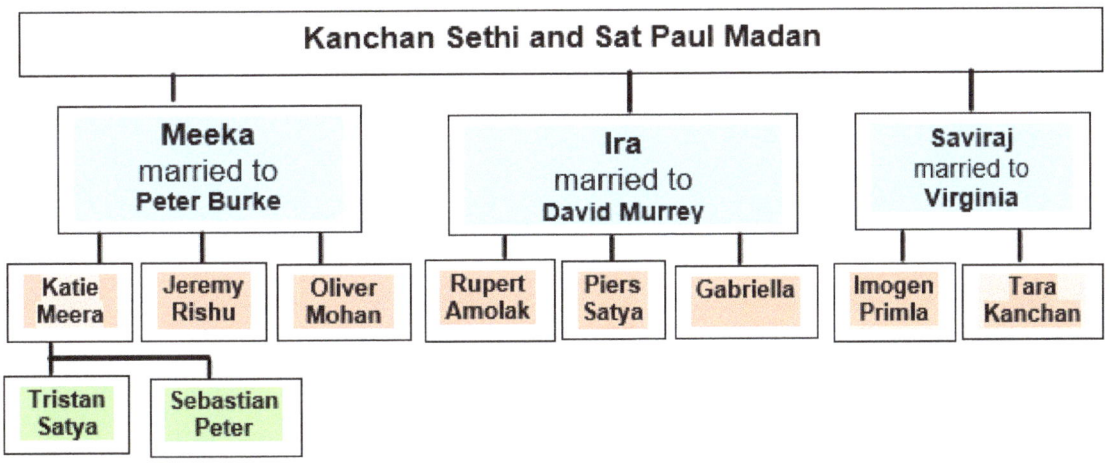

Kanchan Sethi and Sat Paul Madan have three children, **Meeka**, **Ira** and **Saviraj**.

Meeka is the eldest and was born on 24th August 1958 in U.K. and completed her education in UK itself. Meeka married Peter Burke (born on 1st November 1954) on 25th June 1983 in U.K. Meeka is a Chartered Accountant settled in U.K. and has three children Katie Meera, Jeremy Rishu and Oliver Mohan.

Katie Meera, the eldest daughter of Meeka and Peter was born in 1988 and is a doctor by profession. She has two children **Tristan Satya** (born in 2021) and **Sebastian Peter** (born in 2022).

Jeremy Rishu was born in 1990 and is a COO whereas **Oliver Mohan** was born in 1993 and is a Credit Researcher,

Ira was born on 7th November 1961 in U.K. and married David Murrey (born on 26th September 1962) on 5th August 1989. They have three children Rupert Amolak, Piers Satya and Gabriella. **Rupert Amolak** was born in 1994 and is a Civil Servant, **Piers Satya** was born in 1996, is an Artist and **Gabriella** born in 1998 is a HR professional.

Saviraj was born on 20th March 1965. He is a Company Director and is married to Virginia. They have two children, **Imogen Primla** (born in 1999) an entrepreneur and **Tara Kanchan** (born in 2005) who is presently an undergraduate in St. Andrews University.

Kulwant Rai Sethi – Harjas Rai Sethi – Sukhanand Sethi – Ram Krishan Sethi – Dani Ditta Lal Sethi – Narsingh Das Sethi – Ganesh Das Sethi – Amolak Ram Sethi – Yag Sethi

Yag Sethi and Mohini had three children, Amita Sethi, Kapil Sethi and Anil Sethi.

YAG SETHI and FAMILY

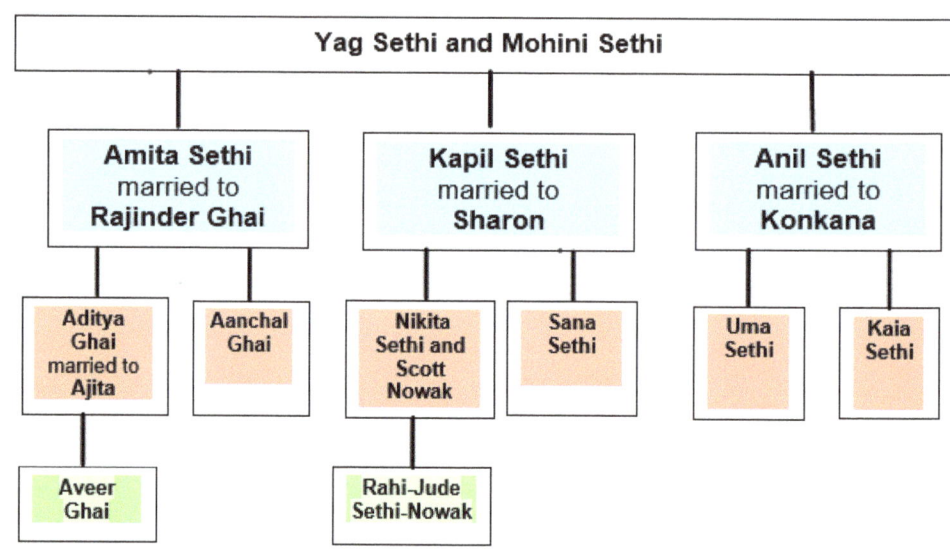

Amita Sethi, the eldest of this families tenth generation was born on 9th November 1958 at Lucknow and had a dynamic upbringing across various Indian cities due to her father's transferable job at Dunlop India Ltd.

Amita completed her schooling at Mater Dei Convent, New Delhi, along with various other institutions across the country.

Her passion for creativity led her to pursue Art Courses in Calcutta, followed by a one-year Secretarial Course, after which she began her professional journey, embarking on a life filled with both personal and professional accomplishments.

Amita's career initially took her into the hospitality industry, where she worked at renowned establishments such as Oberoi Grand, Calcutta, and ITC Hotel Banjara, Hyderabad. However, her artistic inclination steered her toward Gift and Trousseau Packing, a passion she has nurtured since 2009 after completing six months of specialized training. Today, she not only excels as a Gift and Wedding Packer and Trainer but also empowers women by training them to start their own businesses in this field. She is fond of reading, traveling, and exploring new creative ideas in gift packing.

Amita got married to Rajinder Ghai on 10th January 1981 at New Delhi and is now settled there.

Rajinder Ghai was born on June 2, 1953, in New Delhi, Rajinder Ghai received his early education at Delhi Public School, New Delhi, before graduating from Shri Ram College of Commerce (SRCC), New Delhi.

A dedicated entrepreneur, he ventured into the garment export industry, where he has established a strong presence. His work is his passion, and his enthusiasm for the garment business is unmatched, making him a true workaholic who lives and breathes garments, garments, and more garments!

Amita Sethi Ghai and Rajinder have two children **Aditya Ghai** and **Aanchal Ghai**.

Aditya Ghai was born on November 30, 1984, in New York, USA, and followed in his father's footsteps while also carving his own path in the hospitality industry. He completed his schooling at Don Bosco School, New Delhi, before pursuing a degree in Hotel Management from San Jose, California, USA. His career began at The Marriott Hotel in San Jose, where he gained valuable experience before returning to New Delhi, where he is now actively involved in the garment export business.

Aditya's hobbies include traveling and listening to Sufi music, reflecting his love for culture and exploration.

On June 3, 2015, Aditya married Ajita in New Delhi. It is indeed a coincidence that Ajita was born the same day as Aditya i.e. 30th November 1984. Ajita did her schooling at Convent of Jesus and Mary, Shimla after which she graduated with BSC in Business management from IILM.

Being a marketing professional Ajita presently works as a Marketing Consultant while pursuing her hobbies of Traveling, Painting, Sketching and Reading. Aditya and Ajita together welcomed their son **Aveer Ghai** on November 8, 2024, at New Delhi just a day before Amita's birthday.

Aanchal Ghai was born on June 2, 1990, in New Delhi, her father Rajinder too was born on 2nd June – another coincidence.

Aanchal Ghai completed her schooling at Convent of Jesus and Mary, New Delhi, before graduating in Journalism from Kamala Nehru College, New Delhi.

She initially explored the media industry, writing for a daily newspaper, before eventually joining the family garment export business. Now settled in New Delhi, Aanchal enjoys traveling, reading, and music, balancing her creative interests with her professional endeavours. The Ghai family is a perfect blend of creativity, business acumen, and passion. Whether in garment exports, hospitality, or creative arts, they have carved their own paths while supporting and inspiring one another. With their entrepreneurial spirit and love for their respective crafts, they continue to grow and thrive in their fields.

Kapil Sethi was born on 26th April 1963 in Lucknow, India and studied in St. Thomas school, Calcutta. He graduated from Meerut University.

Kapil Sethi is currently the CEO at Net Effect Media in San Jose California. From 1984 – 1999 Kapil was employed with the Taj Group of Hotels, Delhi and Dunlop, Delhi. He moved to the US in 2000 as the CEO of Eros Entertainment.

Kapil Sethi got married to Sharon on 12th December 1987 at New Delhi.

Sharon was born on 21st November 1963 in Bombay, India and studied in Vidyaranya High School, Hyderabad and graduated from Osmania University, Hyderabad.

Sharon is presently the Catering Supervisor – Cupertino Union School District. In India Sharon worked with the Taj Group of Hotels, Sethi Bombay.

Kapil and Sharon are settled in San Jose California and have two daughters. **Nikita Sethi** and **Sana Sethi.**

Nikita Sethi was born at Meerut on 26th September 1991. She studied at Lynbrook High San Jose and De Anza College Cupertino and Oregon State University.

Nikita Sethi is a Communications and Marketing professional working with MisFits aka Imperfect Foods.

She is settled in Tucson Arizona with her partner Scott Nowak and son **Rahi-Jude-Sethi-Nowak**.

Sana Sethi was born on 21st November 1996 at Meerut and studied at Lynbrook High West Valley College and UC Long Beach CA.

Sana Sethi is presently the Communications Manager with SF Rising and is settled in Pacifica, California.

Anil Sethi the youngest in his family, was born on January 2, 1965, in Nagpur.

He completed his schooling in various cities, including Hyderabad, as his father, Yag Sethi, was frequently transferred.

On May 2, Anil married Konkana in New Delhi.

The couple later settled in Canada, where they are raising their two daughters, Kaia Sethi and Uma Sethi.

Kaia Sethi was born on January 2, 2016, in Canada, while **Uma Sethi** was born on December 15, 2021.

Kulwant Rai Sethi – Harjas Rai Sethi – Sukhanand Sethi – Ram Krishan Sethi – Dani Ditta Lal Sethi – Narsingh Das Sethi – Ganesh Das Sethi – Amolak Ram Sethi – Raj Sethi

RAJ SETHI and FAMILY

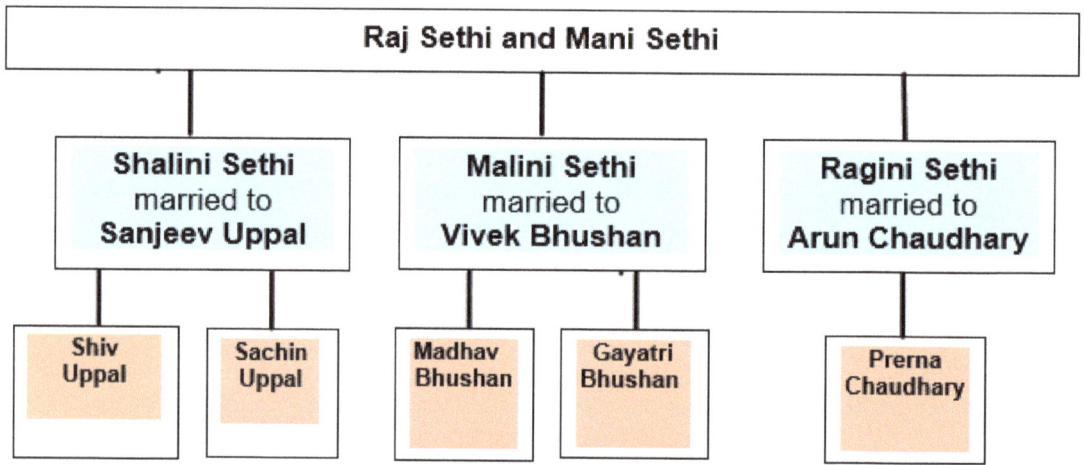

Raj Sethi and Mani have three daughters, **Shalini Sethi, Malini Sethi** and **Ragini Sethi**.

Shalini Sethi was born in New Delhi on 6th July 1966. She studied at Apeejay School and later did an Interior Designing Course and is now a home maker.

Shalini got married to Sanjeev Uppal on 29th November 1987 at New Delhi.

Sanjeev was born in New Delhi on 20th January 1960 and studied at Xavier's Calcutta. He later completed his Chartered Accountancy and is presently leading a comfortable retired life. They are settled in Gurgaon.

Shalini and Sanjeev have two sons **Sachin Uppa**l and **Shiv Uppal**.

Sachin Uppal was born on 12th July 1990 at New Delhi and studied at Doon School. Sachin later completed his MBA from Indian School of Business. He is presently working as a Regional Manager with an FMCG.

Shiv Uppal was born on 15th March 1996 at New Delhi and studied at Cathedral School, Mumbai. He completed his under grad from SMU, Singapore. Shiv is now pursuing his MBA from Emory in Atlanta, USA.

Malini Sethi was born in New Delhi on 14th November 1967 and after her schooling specialised in Fashion Designing

On 12th December 1989, Malini got married to Vivek Bhushan who was born in Delhi on19th July 1960.

Vivek graduated from Shri Ram College of Commerce, Delhi and started a garment export house. Malini and Vivek live in Sainik Farms, New Delhi.

Malini and Vivek have a son, **Madhav** and a daughter **Gayatr**i.

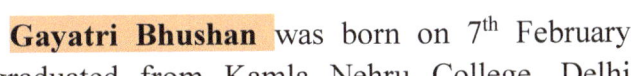

Madhav Bhushan was born on 26th February 1994 at Delhi. He graduated from Kirorimal College, Delhi University and works with TCM Sports – a leading sports management and marketing company specializing in global events and brand partnerships.

Gayatri Bhushan was born on 7th February 1997 at Delhi and graduated from Kamla Nehru College, Delhi University. She is now doing her Masters in Sports and Exercise Physiology from Laughborough University, U.K. Gayatri is a practising sports psychologist and worked for Chelsea Football Club and Brentford Football Club.

Ragini Sethi was born in New Delhi on 10th October 1970. She studied at Apeejay School and completed her graduation in Political Science Honours from Indraprastha University, North Campus New Delhi.

Ragini got married to Arun Chaudhary on 28th April 1997 at Faridabad.

Arun Chaudhary was born at Gorakhpur on 9th March 1968.

He studied at De Nobili School, Dhanbad and later graduated in BCom Honours from GCM Chandigarh.

Arun Chaudhary works for FCM Travel Solutions.

Ragini is a home maker, and they are settled in Bangalore. Ragini and Arun have a daughter, Prerna Chaudhary.

Prerrna Chaudhary was born on 15th January 2000 at New Delhi.

Prerna studied at Presidency School and graduated in BA from Mount Caramel.

Prerna Chaudhary completed her MBA from CMS Business School, Bangalore.

After completing her MBA, Prerna started working with Zomato.

Prerna Chaudhary lives in Bangalore with Ragini and Arun.

Kulwant Rai Sethi – Harjas Rai Sethi – Sukhanand Sethi – Ram Krishan Sethi – Dani Ditta Lal Sethi – Narsingh Das Sethi – Ganesh Das Sethi – Dina Nath Sethi - Janak Sethi

JANAK SETHI (PANT) and FAMILY

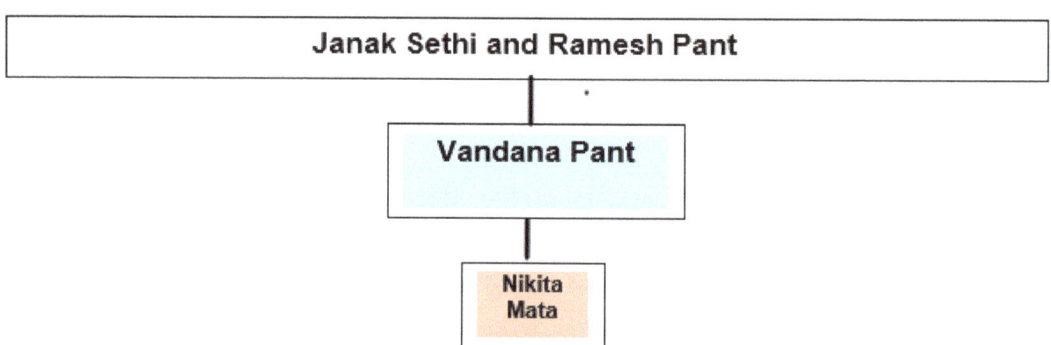

Janak Sethi and Ramesh Pant have a daughter **Vandana Pant**

Vandanna Pant was born on October 29, 1965, in Lucknow, Vandana had her school education in Lucknow and did her B.A. with a major in Psychology from Indraprastha College, Delhi University and Masters in Mass Communication from Jamia Millia University, New Delhi.

Vandana Pant is presently a Healthcare Executive, and settled in the San Francisco Bay Area, USA.

Vandana has a daughter, **Nikita Mata** who was born on May 15, 1992, in Winnipeg, Canada. Nikita completed her undergraduate degree with a major in Public Health from the University of California, Berkley. Nikita is currently doing a post-graduation in Interior Architecture and Design.

SATYA ANAND (CHANDOK) and FAMILY

Kulwant Rai Sethi – Harjas Rai Sethi – Sukhanand Sethi – Ram Krishan Sethi – Dani Ditta Lal Sethi – Narsingh Das Sethi – Ganesh Das Sethi – Susheila Sethi (Anand) – Satya Anand (Chandok)

Satya Anand (Chandok) and K.B. Chandok were the proud parents of two children, Navin Chandok and Anju Chandok.

Navin Chandok was born on 28th January 1945 in Lahore. A few years later, his parents moved to Bombay, where he pursued his education at St. Xavier's College.

After graduation, he joined the family business of auto parts under the banner of Upper India Trading Co.

On 14th May 1972, Navin married Niren, who was born on 4th September 1953 in Amritsar.

Niren completed her schooling at Sacred Hearts High School and later earned a B.Sc. in Home Science from Lady Irwin College, Delhi. After marriage, she pursued a Diploma in Early Childhood Care and Education from Sophia Polytechnic, Bombay and currently teaches at Sophia Nursery School.

Navin and Niren were blessed with two daughters, **Bindiya Chandok** and **Nidhi Chandok**.

Bindiya Chandok was born on 30th January 1973 in Bombay, she studied at Walsingham House School before earning a B.A. in Economics (Honours) from St. Xavier's College, Bombay. She later completed a Diploma in Travel and Tourism from Sophia Polytechnic and worked in a travel agency.

On 18th November 1995, Bindiya married Prateek Majumdar, who was born on 2nd October 1969 in Stockport, U.K. Prateek studied at Cathedral High School, Bombay, graduated from St. Xavier's College, and now runs the renowned JNM Homeo Sadan in Kolkata, a homeopathic polyclinic founded by his grandfather.

Bindiya and Prateek have a daughter, **Meghna Majumdar**, born on 20th February 2002 in London. Meghna completed her schooling at Modern High School, Kolkata, and in 2024, graduated from Bath University, U.K., with a degree in Psychopathy.

Nidhi Chandok was born on 30th May 1979 in Mumbai, Nidhi studied at Walsingham House School and later graduated from St. Xavier's College, Mumbai, specializing in Public Relations Management.

On 24th May 2006, Nidhi Chandok married Rishi Bhasin, who studied at Don Bosco High School, Mumbai, and graduated from Jai Hind College. Rishi is a financier associated with Dara Shaw and Co., Mumbai.

Nidhi Bhasin and Rishi Bhasin have a son, **Suveer Bhasin** born on 22nd February 2012, who is currently studying in Grade 8 at Don Bosco International School, Mumbai.

Anju Chandok, the younger sister of Navin Chandok was born on 4th November 1946 in Bombay.

Anju Chandok studied at Queen Mary High School and married Arun Hari in Delhi on 24th April 1966. The late Arun Hari was a pharmacist and the proprietor of R.B. Hamer and Co., a leading chemist and general merchant company based in Dehradun.

Anju Hari and Arun Hari were blessed with three children, Anu Hari, Rohit Hari and Gayatri Har.

Anu Hari is married to Rajnish Mehta, and they have two children, **Raghav Mehta** and **Devika Mehta**.

Rohit Hari is married to Malika, and they have two daughters, **Niharika Hari** and **Tarini Hari**.

Gayatri Hari is married to Udai Java, and they have a daughter, **Akansha Java** and a son, **Arjun Java**.

SATISH ANAND and FAMILY

Kulwant Rai Sethi – Harjas Rai Sethi – Sukhanand Sethi – Ram Krishan Sethi – Dani Ditta Lal Sethi – Narsingh Das Sethi – Ganesh Das Sethi – Susheila Sethi (Anand) – Satish Anand

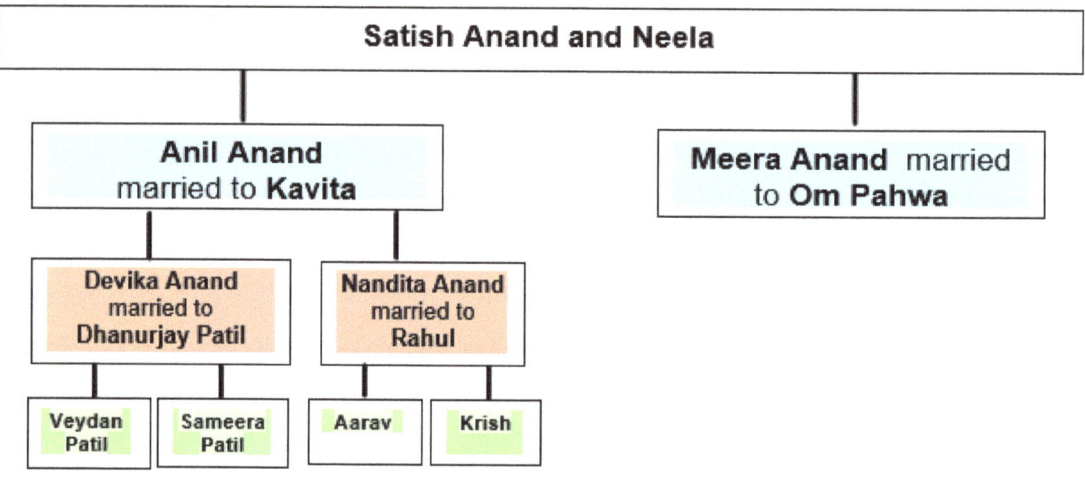

Satish Anand and Neela were blessed with a son, Anil Anand, and a daughter, Meera Anand.

Anil Anand was born in Los_Angeles, USA. He briefly studied at Doon School in Dehradun before continuing his education in Bombay. He later graduated from the University of Manchester.

After completing his studies, Anil joined his father's plastic chemicals business in Mumbai.

Anil Anand married Kavita in Bombay, and the couple later relocated to the USA, where they had two daughters, Devika Anand and Nandita Anand.

Devika Anand married Dhanurjay Patil, and they were blessed with two children, **Veydan Patil** and **Sameera Patil**.

Nandita Anandi married Rahul, and they had two sons, **Aarav** and **Krish**.

Satish and Neela's younger daughter, **Meera Anand** was born in Bombay. After completing her education, she married Om Pahwa.

USHA ANAND (CHADHA) and FAMILY

Kulwant Rai Sethi – Harjas Rai Sethi – Sukhanand Sethi – Ram Krishan Sethi – Dani Ditta Lal Sethi – Narsingh Das Sethi – Ganesh Das Sethi – Susheila Sethi – Usha Anand (Chadha)

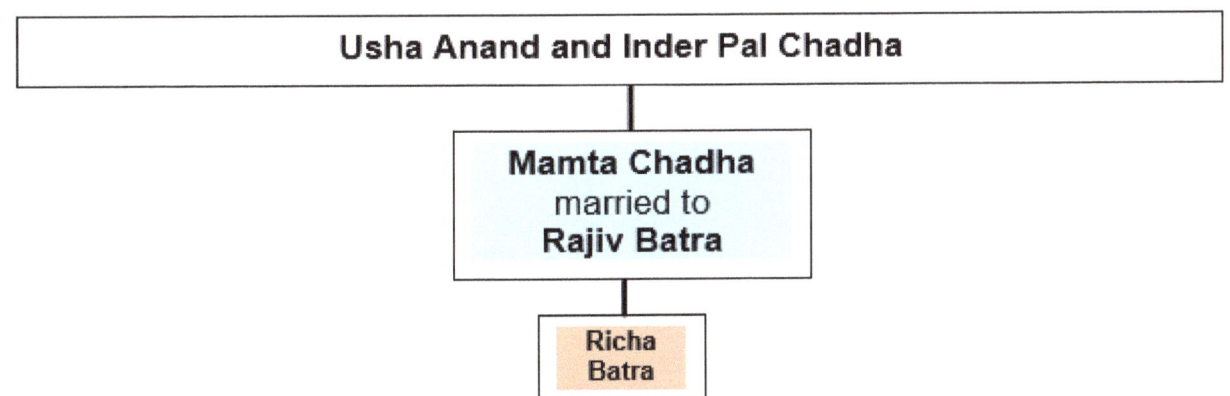

Usha Anand and Inder Pal Chadha are the proud parents of their daughter, **Mamta. Batra.**

Mamta was born in Delhi on February 13, 1959. She completed her schooling at the Convent of Jesus and Mary, Delhi, before earning a B.A. (Hons.) in Political Science from Gargi College, Delhi University. She married Rajiv Batra on October 6, 1984, in Delhi.

Rajiv Batra was born on September 30, 1955, in Bokaro, Bihar. He studied at St. Xaviers, Delhi, and went on to graduate with an Economics (Hons.) degree from Shri Ram College of Commerce.

He also qualified as a Chartered Accountant. Over the years, Rajiv held key positions in leading organizations, working with Xerox in the USA and later serving as CFO at Xerox in Delhi. He then joined Digital India as CFO and subsequently moved to Cummins India as their CFO, based in Pune. After 20 years of service, he retired from Cummins and is now engaged in film distribution across the UAE and other Middle Eastern countries. Mamta and Rajiv are now settled in Pune.

Mamta and Rajiv Batra have a daughter, Richa Batra, born on February 17, 1987, in Delhi. Richa completed her schooling in Bangalore and at CJM, Delhi. She later earned a B.B.A. from Symbiosis, Pune, followed by an MBA from the Symbiosis Institute of Business Management, Pune. Now based in Mumbai, she works as a Senior Manager (Marketing) with VISA.

PRAMILA ANAND and FAMILY

Kulwant Rai Sethi – Harjas Rai Sethi – Sukhanand Sethi – Ram Krishan Sethi – Dani Ditta Lal Sethi – Narsingh Das Sethi – Ganesh Das Sethi – Susheila Sethi – Pramila Anand (Trehan)

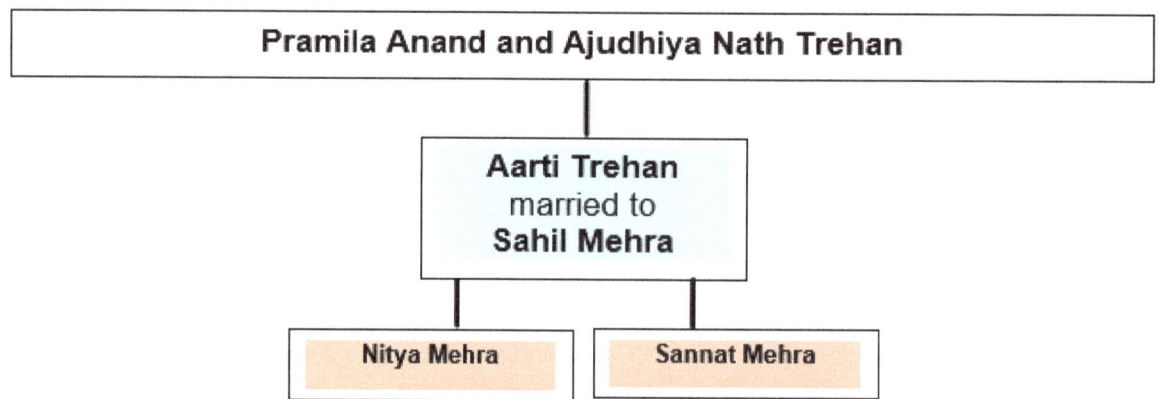

Pramila Anand and Ajudhiya Nath Trehan were the proud parents of their only daughter, Aarti Trehan born on January 3, 1968, in New Delhi,

Aarti pursued her early education at Mater Dei Convent in Delhi and KVM in Ludhiana before completing her graduation from Punjab University. Passionate about academics, she began teaching at a school after graduation and continued to nurture young minds until her marriage.

On September 6, 1997, Aarti Trehan married Sahil Mehra in New Delhi.

Sahil was born on October 30, 1965, in New Delhi. He studied at Happy School in Delhi and later graduated with an Eco (Hons) degree from Shri Ram College of Commerce, Delhi University.

Sahil is an entrepreneur in the garment export industry and also serves as the country manager for an American garment company.

Aarti and Sahil are blessed with two children, **Nitya Mehra** and **Sannat Mehra**. The family resides between Gurgaon and New Delhi.

Nitya Mehra was born on June 10, 1998, in Delhi. She completed her schooling at Heritage School, Delhi, and earned her degree from Amity University, Noida. She is currently based in Gurgaon, working as a Campaign Manager (Marketing) with ETS IT Solutions, an American IT company.

Sannat Mehra was born on November 3, 2003, in New Delhi. He also attended Heritage School, Delhi, and is currently in his final year of a BBA (Marketing) program at NMIMS, Mumbai.

SUDHIR ANAND and FAMILY

Kulwant Rai Sethi – Harjas Rai Sethi – Sukhanand Sethi – Ram Krishan Sethi – Dani Ditta Lal Sethi – Narsingh Das Sethi – Ganesh Das Sethi – Susheila Sethi (Anand) – Sudhir Anand

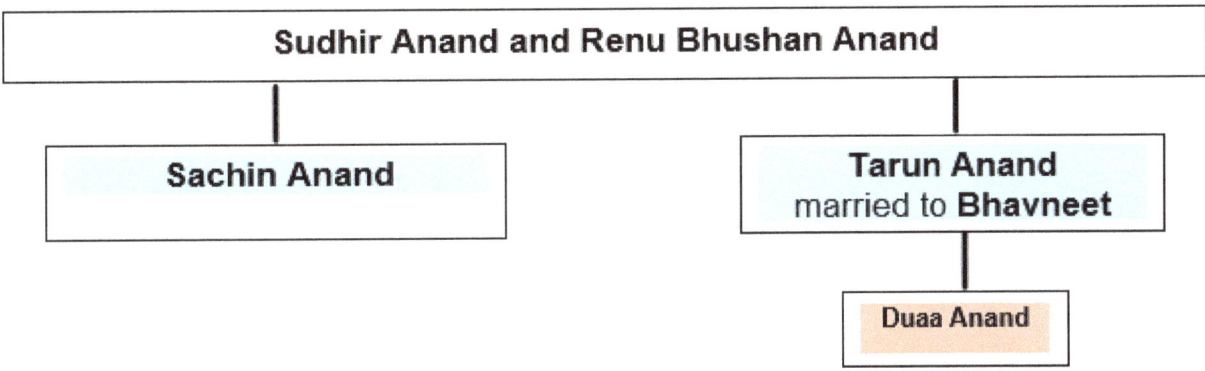

Sudhir Anand and Renu are the proud parents of two sons, Sachin Anand and Tarun Anand.

Sachin Anand was born on May 1, 1975, in Delhi. He completed his schooling at Green House High School in Mumbai and went on to earn a B. Com degree from Jai hind College, Mumbai. He also pursued a diploma in Finance from K.C. College, Mumbai.

During his college years, Sachin worked as a Marketing Executive with "My Own Chocolates." After graduating, he joined Internet Resources Pvt. Ltd. (My India – Hungama) as a Marketing Executive and later expanded his expertise into event management.

He then moved to Result McCann as a Senior Account Executive, where he played a key role in conceptualizing, producing, and executing the Raymonds Fashion Show in India—an event that laid the foundation for India's Fashion Week.

Building on this success, Sachin joined Ogilvy as a Group Account Manager and later spent 15 years at JWT – Wunderman Thompson, eventually rising to the position of Vice President. He then took on the role of Senior Vice President at Rediffusion Brand Solutions.

A passionate animal lover and devoted dog enthusiast, Sachin ultimately transitioned into the pet care industry. He joined Crown Veterinary Services to help establish a nationwide chain of pet clinics dedicated to the well-being of animals.

Tarun Anand was born on August 24, 1978, in Bombay. He attended Greenlawn's High School and later earned a Bachelor of Commerce degree from H.R. College of Commerce and Economics. He also got a degree in Graphic and Animation.

After graduation, he worked as a Graphic Designer at Cinevistas and in event management with Wizcraft Entertainment before moving to Toronto, Canada. Currently, he serves as the Store Manager at Napa Auto Parts in Toronto.

On July 6, 2008, Tarun married Bhavneet Anand in Mumbai.

Bhavneet was born on April 24, 1984, in Bombay to Charanjit Singh Anand and Kavaljeet Kaur Anand.

She completed her schooling at Bombay Scottish School and graduated with a degree in English Literature from Mumbai University. Following her marriage, she relocated to Canada, where she worked with Dream Party Décor.

On January 4, 2025, Tarun and Bhavneet welcomed their daughter and Oreo welcomed his little sister **Duaa Anand**.

DAMAN BHASIN and FAMILY

Kulwant Rai Sethi – Harjas Rai Sethi – Sukhanand Sethi – Ram Krishan Sethi – Dani Ditta Lal Sethi – Narsingh Das Sethi – Ganesh Das Sethi – Raj Dulari Bhasin – Daman Bhasin

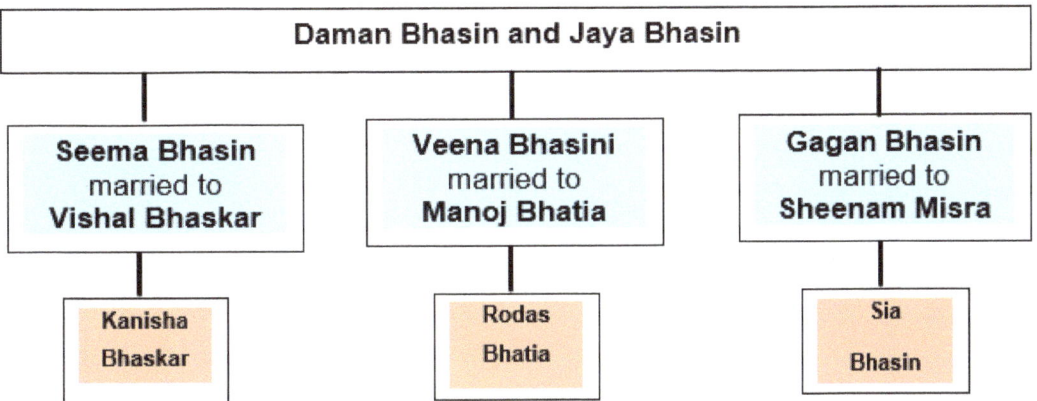

Daman and Jaya Bhasin were blessed with three children, **Seema Bhasin, Veena Bhasin** and **Gagan Bhasin**.

Seema Bhasin was born in 1972 in Ambala and pursued her education in Dehradun, where her parents were posted.

Seema Bhasin married Vishal Bhaskar in 1998, and they were blessed with a daughter, Kanisha Bhaskar born in October 2001.

Kanisha is currently pursuing her post-graduation in London.

Tragically, Seema passed away when Kanisha was still very young.

Veena Bhasin was born in 1976 in Assam, where her father was stationed at the time.

She completed her education in Dehradun and married Manoj Bhatia in 2004.

They have a son, Rodas Bhatia, born in October 2008, who is currently studying at a boarding school in Mussoorie.

Veena is a homemaker.

Gagan Bhasin was born in 1978 in Assam and completed his schooling in Dehradun before pursuing an engineering degree in Maharashtra.

Gagan Bhasin is a Telecom Engineer working in Gurgaon.

Gagan Bhasin married Sheenam Misra in 2009.

Gagan Bhasin and Sheenam have a daughter, Sia Bhasin.

Sia Bhasin was born in February 2011 and is currently studying in Gurgaon.

The family is settled in Gurgaon.

ASHWANI BHASIN and FAMILY

Kulwant Rai Sethi – Harjas Rai Sethi – Sukhanand Sethi – Ram Krishan Sethi – Dani Ditta Lal Sethi – Narsingh Das Sethi – Ganesh Das Sethi – Raj Dulari Bhasin - Ashwani Bhasin

Ashwani Kumar Bhasin and Jyoti were blessed with three children—two sons and a daughter.

Their eldest son, **Rajiv Bhasin** was born on June 11, 1984, in Ahmedabad. He studied at the Institute of Hotel Management in Meerut and is now an entrepreneur settled in Gurugram.

Sanjeev Bhasin was born on May 31, 1986, in Ambala, Haryana. He earned a B. Com degree from S.D. College, Ambala, followed by an MBA from Alliance Business School, Bangalore. He married Aditi Gupta, who was born on January 7, 1987, in Delhi. Aditi completed her BBA and MBA from Bhartiya Vidyapeeth, Delhi.

Sanjeev Bhasin and Aditi Bhasin were blessed with a daughter, **Meher Bhasin** born on 15th June 1920 at Gurugram. Meher Bhasin is presently studying in DPS, Gurugram. Sanjeev Bhasin is working with Sun Life Financials as Sr. Manager, Administration and Aditi Bhasin works as Associate Manager – HR with Nagarro Software's and are happily settled in Gurugram.

The youngest sibling, **Shelika Bhasin** was born on October 23, 1991, in Ambala, Haryana. She completed her B. Tech in Electronics and Communication Engineering (ECE) from Kurukshetra University. Shelika is currently working as Manager – HR and Operations at Noble House Consulting India Pvt. Ltd., Gurugram.

KAMLESH BHASIN and FAMILY

Kulwant Rai Sethi – Harjas Rai Sethi – Sukhanand Sethi – Ram Krishan Sethi – Dani Ditta Lal Sethi – Narsingh Das Sethi – Ganesh Das Sethi – Raj Dulari Bhasin - Kamlesh Bhasin

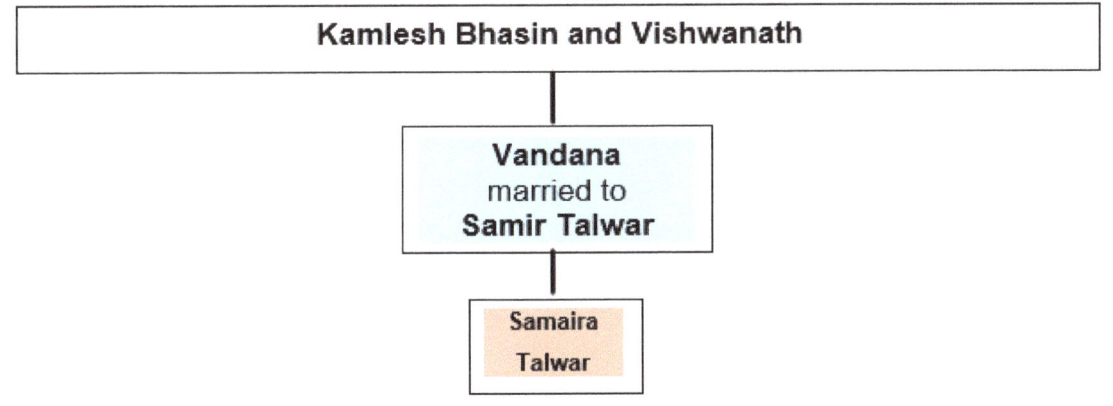

Kamlesh Bhasin and Vishwanath were blessed with their only daughter, Vandana.

Vandana was born on December 30, 1975, in Ambala. She completed her schooling at Air Force School, Ambala Cantt, and graduated from S.D. College, Kurukshetra University. With a keen interest in teaching, she pursued a B.Ed. from Jammu University and later earned an M.Phil. in English from Manipal University. She began her teaching career at Golden Public School (Don Bosco) and later joined Cecil Convent School.

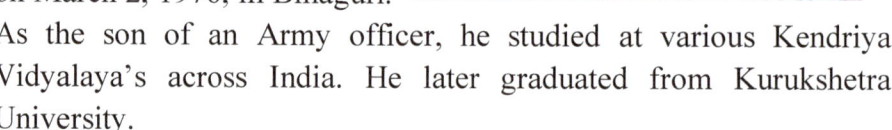

On February 6, 2003, Vandana married Samir Talwar in Ambala Cantt. Samir was born on March 2, 1976, in Binaguri. As the son of an Army officer, he studied at various Kendriya Vidyalaya's across India. He later graduated from Kurukshetra University.

Vandana and Samir were blessed with a daughter, **Samaira Talwar** born on January 4, 2006, in Ambala. Samaira completed her schooling at Cecil Convent School, Ambala, and is currently pursuing a degree in Economics at the University of British Columbia, Kelowna Campus, in Vancouver.

Vandana is presently the Principal of Roots Public School, Ambala Cantt, while Samir serves as the Zonal Head (North) at ICICI Bank.

Vandana and Samir are settled in Ambala Cantt.

VIJAY BHASIN and FAMILY

Kulwant Rai Sethi – Harjas Rai Sethi – Sukhanand Sethi – Ram Krishan Sethi – Dani Ditta Lal Sethi – Narsingh Das Sethi – Ganesh Das Sethi – Raj Dulari Bhasin - Vijay Bhasin

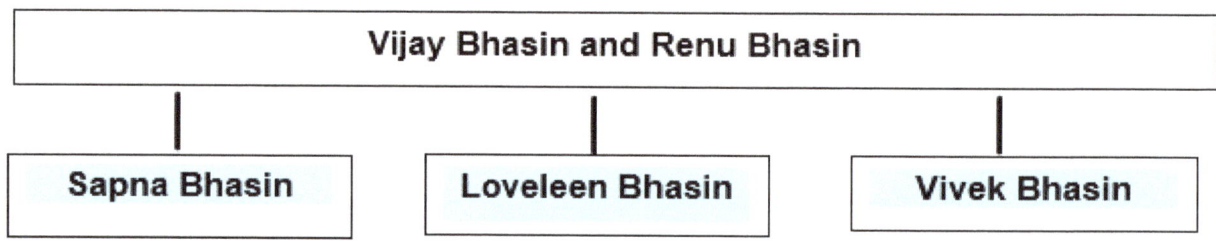

Vijay Bhasin and Renu Bhasin are blessed with three children—two daughters and a son.

Their eldest daughter, **Sapna Bhasin**, was born on December 15, 1989, and is currently working for an emigration company.

Loveleen Bhasin born on July 7, 1991, is a Chartered Accountant and works with a Chartered Accountancy firm.

The youngest, **Vivek Bhasin** was born on July 7, 1994. After completing his schooling, he earned an MBA and is now employed with a private organization.

VINAY BHASIN and FAMILY

Kulwant Rai Sethi – Harjas Rai Sethi – Sukhanand Sethi – Ram Krishan Sethi – Dani Ditta Lal Sethi – Narsingh Das Sethi – Ganesh Das Sethi – Raj Dulari Bhasin - Vinay Bhasin

Vinay Bhasin and Anju Bhasin

|
Ansh Bhasin

Vinay Bhasin and Anju Bhasin are blessed with their only son, **Ansh Bhasin. Ansh Bhasin** was born on December 24, 2006. He is currently studying in Ambala.

MANJULA SETHI and FAMILY

Kulwant Rai Sethi – Harjas Rai Sethi – Sukhanand Sethi – Ram Krishan Sethi – Dani Ditta Lal Sethi – Narsingh Das Sethi – Ganesh Das Sethi – Chamanlal Sethi – Manjula Sethi (Kumar)

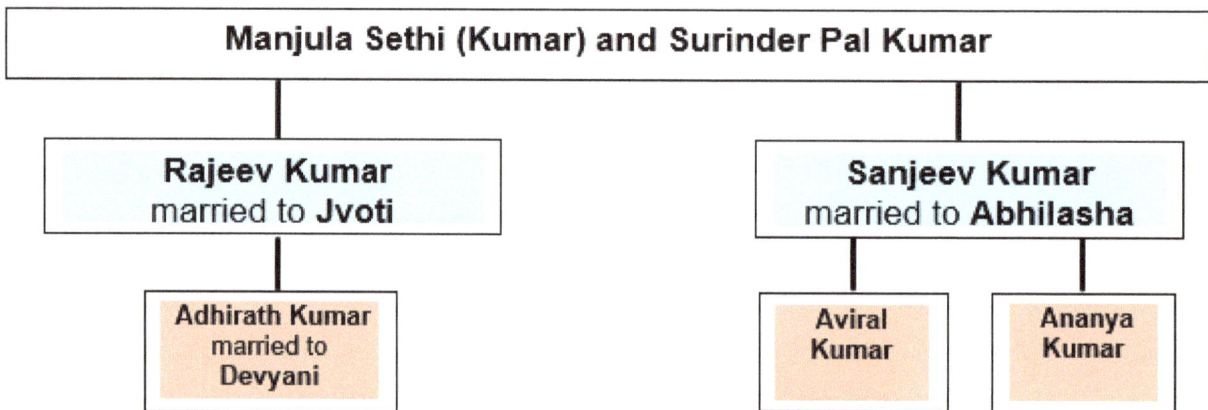

Manjula Sethi (Kumar) and Surinder Pal Kumar have two sons, Rajeev Kumar and Sanjeev Kumar.

Rajeev Kumar (Sunny) was born on 18th March 1963 in Bhopal. He completed his schooling at Campion School, Bhopal, and earned both his B.Sc. and M.Sc. degrees from Safia College, Bhopal. Rajeev began his career with Avery India before joining his younger brother's business in IT and software. Currently, Rajeev owns a Godrej Interio franchise in Bhopal.

On 12th October 1989, Rajeev married Jyoti Wahie in Agra. Jyoti was born on 19th November 1966 and completed her schooling at St. George's School, Agra. She later specialized in Home Science at the Home Science Institute, Agra. Before her marriage, Jyoti worked with Mughal Sheraton, Agra, and after relocating to Bhopal, she began teaching at Sanskar Valley School.

Rajeev and Jyoti have a son, **Adirath Kumar**, born on 30th March 1991 in Bhopal. Adhirath completed his schooling at Campion School, Bhopal, and pursued Marine Engineering at Vels Institute of Maritime Studies. He is currently serving as a 2nd Officer in the Merchant Navy.

On 2nd July 2021, Adhirath married Devyani Thakur, who was born on 10th December 1992 in Bhopal. Devyani completed her schooling at Carmel Convent School, Bhopal, and earned an MBA from IPER Institute of Management, Bhopal. She previously worked with Axis Bank and is now employed at Sanfield India Limited, Bhopal.

Sanjeev Kumar (Winnie) was born on November 13, 1964, in Bhopal. He completed his schooling at Campion School, Bhopal, and later graduated in Electronic Engineering from Sardar Vallabhbhai Polytechnic, Bhopal.

Sanjeev began his career at Bradma, where he worked for two years before joining Lloyd Insulation. With a strong interest in electronics, he ventured into his own business in 1987, specialising in IT products

and software, based in Bhopal and later converted it into a Pvt. Limited Company, ITSC Technologies Pvt. Ltd. of which he is the CEO.

On November 29, 1992, Sanjeev married Abhilasha Tarneja in Bhopal.

Abhilasha, born on March 17, 1968, in Jhansi, attended Scindia Kanya Vidyalaya in Gwalior for her schooling and completed her M. Tech from

BUIT Barkatullah University, Bhopal. She began her career as a teacher at Shri Satya Sai Girls College in Bhopal and retired as the CEO of the institution. Abhilasha is now a blogger and after studying 'Managing Happiness" from Harvard University and 'life Coaching" is a practising counsellor in psychology. She continues to pursue her passions for theatre and painting.

Sanjeev and Abhilasha are settled in Bhopal and are the proud parents of two children, Aviral Kumar and Ananya Kumar.

Aviral Kumar, was born on May 28, 1994, in Bhopal.

Aviral attended Campion School, Bhopal, for his schooling before completing his BTech from PESIT, Bangalore, and MTech from CMU, Pittsburgh, USA. Aviral Kumar currently works as a researcher in DNA in Bangalore.

Ananya Kumar, born exactly four years later on May 28, 1998, in Bhopal, completed her schooling at DPS, Bhopal, and graduated from Fergusson College, Pune.

Ananya Kumar is currently employed with a recruitment company in Dublin.

REENA SETHI and FAMILY

Kulwant Rai Sethi – Harjas Rai Sethi – Sukhanand Sethi – Ram Krishan Sethi – Dani Ditta Lal Sethi – Narsingh Das Sethi – Ganesh Das Sethi – Chamanlal Sethi – Reena Sethi

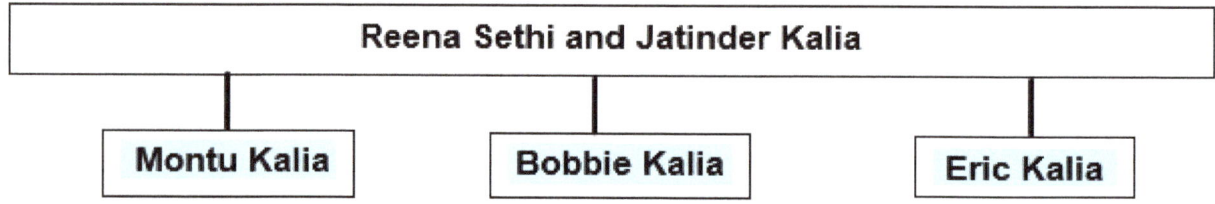

Reena Sethi and Jatinder Kalia have three sons, **Montu Kalia**, **Bobbie Kalia** and **Eric Kalia**.

MINAKSHI SETHI and FAMILY

Kulwant Rai Sethi – Harjas Rai Sethi – Sukhanand Sethi – Ram Krishan Sethi – Dani Ditta Lal Sethi – Narsingh Das Sethi – Ganesh Das Sethi – Chamanlal Sethi – Minakshi Sethi

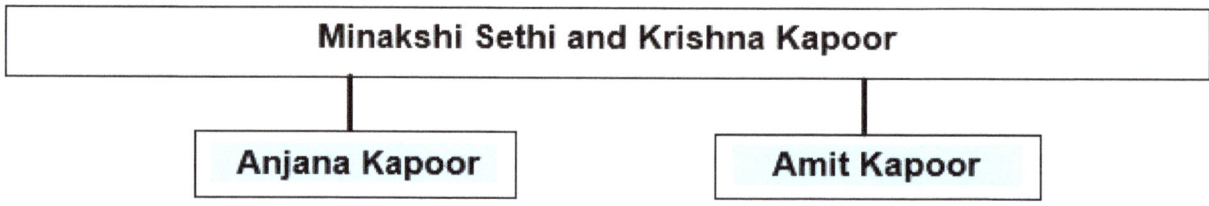

Minakshi Setrgii and Krishna Kapoor have a daughter, **Anjanan Kapoor** and a son, **Amit Kapoor**.

ARUN SETHI and FAMILY

Kulwant Rai Sethi – Harjas Rai Sethi – Sukhanand Sethi – Ram Krishan Sethi – Dani Ditta Lal Sethi – Narsingh Das Sethi – Ganesh Das Sethi – Chamanlal Sethi – Arun Sethi

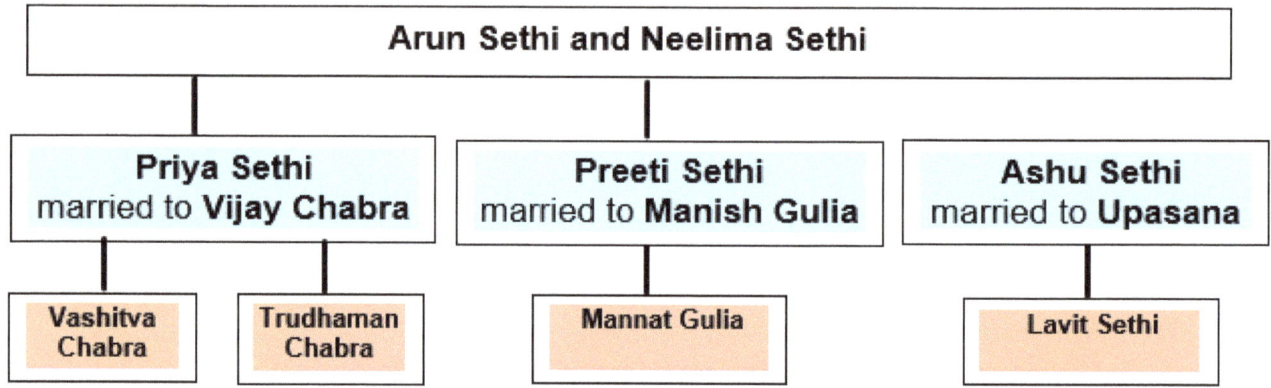

Arun Sethi and Neelima have three children: two daughters, **Priya Sethi** and **Preeti Sethi**, and a son, **Aashu Sethi**.

Priya Sethi was born on November 12, 1977, in Moradabad. She completed her schooling at St. Mary's Convent in Moradabad and later pursued her MA in English Literature from Hindu College, Moradabad. Priya now owns a coaching establishment in Moradabad where she teaches English to students.

On the auspicious day of Baisakhi, January 14, 1999, Priya married Vijay Chabra in Moradabad. Vijay Chabra has a background in hotel management and manages the family business, a chain of hotels. He is also an exporter of brass items and artifacts manufactured in Moradabad.

Priya Chabra and Vijay Chabra have two sons: Vashitya and Tridhaman.

Vashitya Chabraa was born on July 18, 2001, in Moradabad. He completed his schooling in Moradabad and specialized in the IT sector. He is currently based in Canada, working in the Petroleum Industry's IT department.

Tridhaman Chabra was born on January 27, 2011 and is currently studying in Moradabad.

Preeti Sethi was born on February 1, 1979, in Moradabad. After completing her schooling at St. Mary's Convent in Moradabad, she earned a degree in Company Secretary from Delhi University.

On May 11, 2003, Preeti married Capt. Manish Gulia in Moradabad. Manish Gulia, born on February 27, 1975, in Delhi, served in the Indian Army and retired as a Colonel. He is now working as a consultant for the International Olympiad of English Language in Delhi. With a keen interest in horticulture and agriculture, Preeti Gulia established her own industry specializing in Hydroponic Farming in Gurgaon. Preeti and Manish are blessed with a daughter, **Mannat Gulia**, born on March 15, 2014, who is currently studying.

Aashu Sethi was born on February 19, 1983, in Kuwait. He completed his schooling in Moradabad before earning an engineering degree in Ghaziabad. Aashu began his career with Tata Consultancy Services in Noida and later moved to Canada, where he established his own IT consultancy firm. He is now settled in Calgary, Canada.

On April 23, 2014, Aashu Sethi married Upasana, who was born on March 24, 1988, in the Andaman and Nicobar Islands, where her father served as the Labour Commissioner. After completing her schooling, Upasana pursued a specialization in fabric design and currently works with Lululemon, a Canadian multinational apparel brand.

Aashu and Upasana are proud parents to their son, **Lavit Sethi**, who was born on December 21, 2015, in Lamington, UK. And is presently studying in school.

ANOOP SABHARWAL and FAMILY

Kulwant Rai Sethi – Harjas Rai Sethi – Sukhanand Sethi – Ram Krishan Sethi – Dani Ditta Lal Sethi – Narsingh Das Sethi – Ganesh Das Sethi – Kaushalya Sethi (Sabharwal) – Anoop Sabharwal

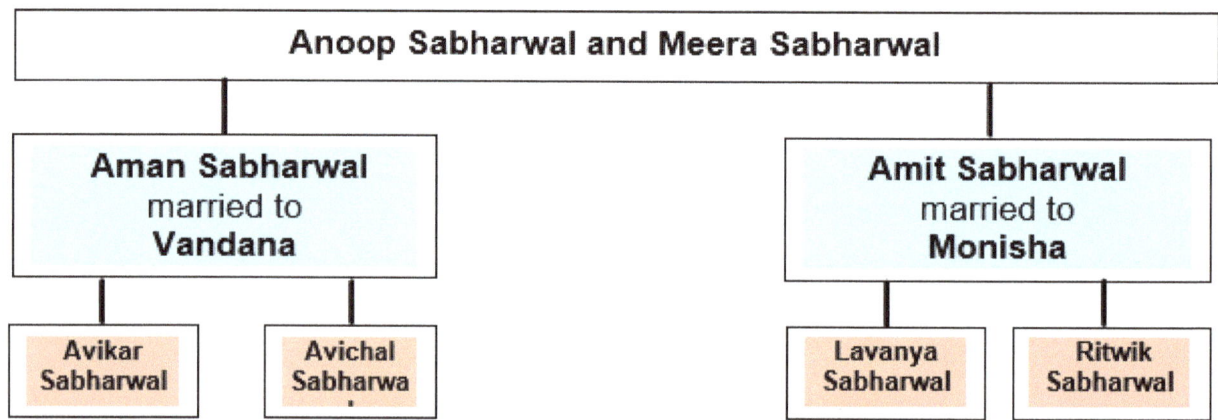

Anoop Sabharwal and Meera Sabharwal have two sons, **Aman Sabharwal** and **Amit Sabharwal**.

Aman Sabharwal the elder son, was born on 2nd October 1968 in Bombay. He pursued his education in Bombay, Coimbatore, and Delhi.

After his schooling, he followed in his father's footsteps and joined the National Defence Academy in January 1986.

Commissioned into the Indian Navy on 1st January 1990, Aman specialized in Naval Operations, Navigation, and Aircraft Direction. Over the course of his distinguished career, he commanded INS Sharabh and played a key role in the 2011 Presidential Fleet Review, earning commendation from the Chief of Naval Staff.

He subsequently served in various strategic roles, including in the Directorate of Naval Operations at Naval Headquarters, as an Officer on Special Duty in the Ministry of External Affairs, and as a Research Fellow at the Institute of Defence Studies and Analysis, focusing on the Indian Ocean Region.

Aman Sabharwal's final posting was as the Naval Control Shipping Officer at the Western Naval Command Headquarters. After more than three decades of service, Aman Sabharwal retired on 31st October 2022 and settled in his ancestral home in Dehradun.

Aman married Vandana on 30th April 1995 in Delhi.

Vandana was born on 19th August 1970 in Neemuch, Madhya Pradesh, Vandana Sabharwal is a highly regarded educator in Social Studies and English, with nearly three decades of teaching experience. She last served as the Principal of the Naval School in Karanja, Mumbai.

Aman and Vandana are the proud parents of their sons, Avikar and Avichal.

Avikar Sabharwal, born on August 31, 1997, is a Chemical Engineer with a postgraduate degree from the Netherlands.

Avikar Sabharwal is currently settled in the Netherlands and works for a company specializing in setting up plants that convert waste into energy.

His younger brother, **Avichar Sabharwal**, was born on October 6, 1999. Avichar Sabharwal is an investment banker currently employed with an American company in Mumbai.

He will soon be moving to the United States to pursue an MBA in Finance at the Darden School of Business, University of Virginia.

Aman Sabharwal the younger son of Anoop and Meera Sabharwal and younger brother of Aman Sabharwal was born on July 13, 1970, and is the founder of '*RedDoorz*', a company based in Singapore.

Aman Sabharwal now resides in Mandurah, Perth, Australia.

Amit Sabharwal got married to Monisha, who has had a long career in the banking sector. Monisha has now taken a sabbatical.

Amit Sabharwal and Monisha Sabharwal are proud parents of two children, **Lavanya** and **Ritwik**.

Lavanya Sabharwal studied Economics in Milan, Italy, and currently works for a consulting firm in Singapore.

Ritwik Sabharwal, the younger son of Amit Sabharwal and Monisha Sabharwal is pursuing a degree in Psychology at the University of Perth, Australia.

UMA SABHARWAL (Kapur) and FAMILY

Kulwant Rai Sethi – Harjas Rai Sethi – Sukhanand Sethi – Ram Krishan Sethi – Dani Ditta Lal Sethi – Narsingh Das Sethi – Ganesh Das Sethi – Kaushalya Sethi (Sabharwal) – Uma Sabharwal

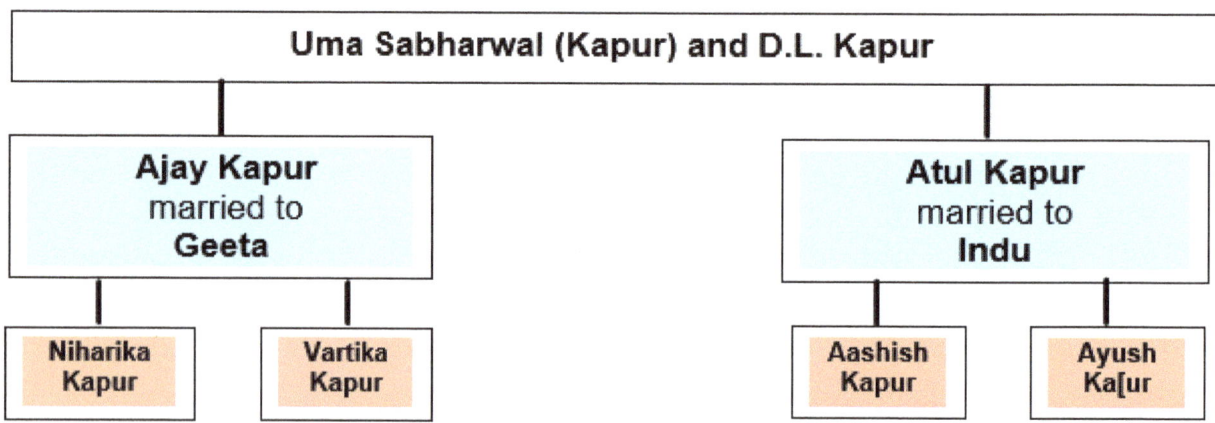

Uma and F.L. Kapur have two sons, **Ajay Kapur** and **Atul Kapur**.

Ajay Kapur got married to Geeta Kapur and the couple are blessed with two daughters, **Niharika Kapur** and **Vartika Kapur**.

Atul Kapur got married to Indu Kapur and the couple are blessed with two sons, **Aashish Kapur** and **Ayush Kapur**.

RAKSHA SABHARWAL (SETHI) and FAMILY

Kulwant Rai Sethi – Harjas Rai Sethi – Sukhanand Sethi – Ram Krishan Sethi – Dani Ditta Lal Sethi – Narsingh Das Sethi – Ganesh Das Sethi – Kaushalya Sethi – Raksha Sabharwal (Sethi)

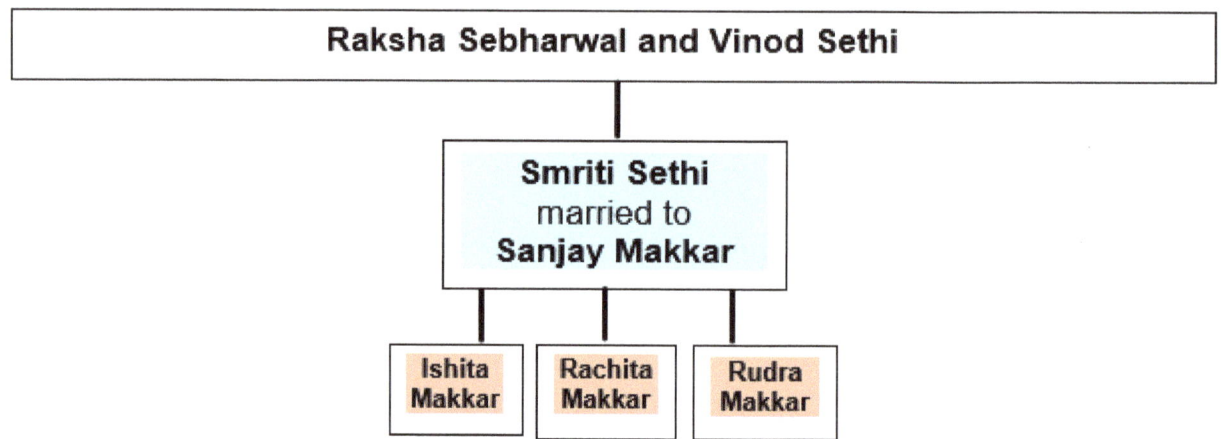

Raksha Sabharwal and Vinod Sethi are the proud parents of their only daughter, **Smriti Sethi**, born on October 16, 1980, in New Delhi.

Smriti completed her early education in Delhi, Gurgaon, and Faridabad before graduating from Delhi University.

On April 14, 2010, Smriti married Sanjay Makkar in Faridabad. Sanjay, born on October 16, 1979, in Gudha, Haryana, studied in both Gudha and Faridabad and later graduated from Kurukshetra University.

Both Smriti and Sanjay began their careers in the Travel and Tourism industry - Smriti worked with Thomas Cook, while Sanjay worked with Swiss Holidays.

Driven by their shared passion for travel, the couple launched their own businesses during the Covid pandemic. Smriti founded an inbound travel company, *Distinct Destinations'*, while Sanjay established an outbound travel company, '*Star world'*.

Smriti and Sanjay are blessed with three children: **Ishita Makkar**, born on March 28, 2011, who is currently in 10th grade, **Rachita Makkar**, born on October 14, 2015, who is in 5th grade and their son, **Rudra Makka**, born on October 5, 2017, who is in the 3rd grade. The family is happily settled in Faridabad.

RAJAN SAWHNEY and FAMILY

Kulwant Rai Sethi – Harjas Rai Sethi – Sukhanand Sethi – Ram Krishan Sethi – Dani Ditta Lal Sethi – Narsingh Das Sethi – Ganesh Das Sethi – Lakhwanti Sethi – Rajan Sawhney.

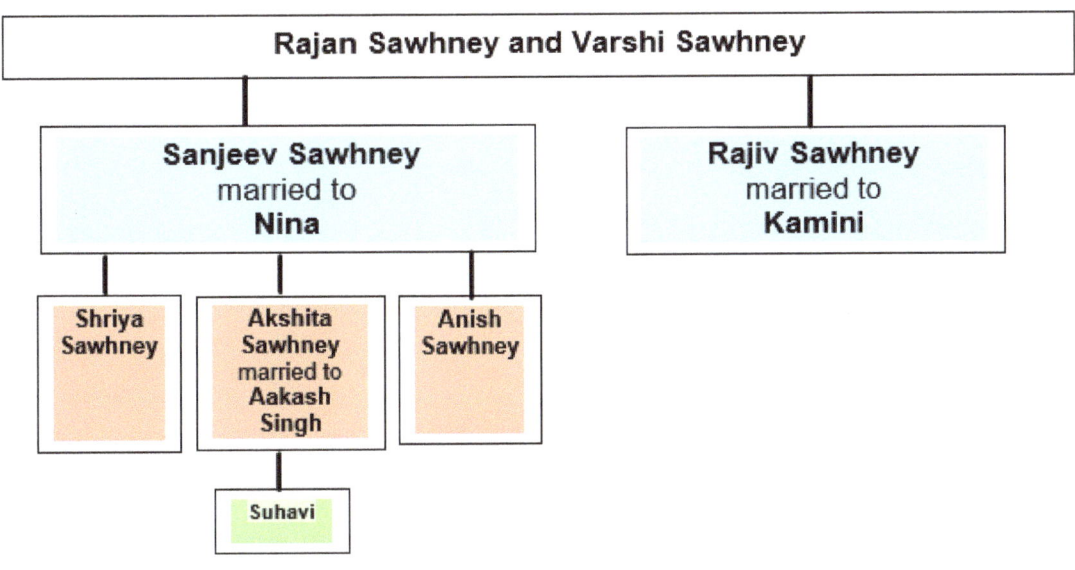

Rajan Sawhney and Varshi Sawhney had two sons, **Sanjeev Sawhney** and **Rajiv Sawhney**.

Sanjeev Sawhney was born on July 11, 1957, in Amritsar. He completed his schooling in Chandigarh and pursued higher education at Punjab University, earning a Bachelor of Arts (B.A.) degree followed by a Master of Arts (M.A.). Sanjeev began his career with Usha Sriram Pistons before establishing his own business as an authorized agent for various companies, supplying goods to both government and private sector undertakings.

On February 13, 1986, Sanjeev married Nina in Chandigarh. Born in Punjab, Nina completed her postgraduation with an M.A. and later earned a doctorate (Ph.D.). She built a successful academic career, serving as the principal of a college in Chandigarh.

Sanjeev and Nina have three children: two daughters, Shriya Sawhney and Akshita Sawhney, and a son, Anish Sawhney.

Shriya Sawhney is a renowned Tarot Card Reader and runs a consultancy business in Chandigarh.

Akshita Sawhney specializes in the French language and teaches French in Chandigarh. She is married to Aakash, and they are blessed with a daughter, **Suhavi**.

Anish Sawhney completed his studies in Chandigarh and later ventured into real estate. He is currently a Real Estate Consultant based in Chandigarh.

Sanjeev Sawhney was born on December 18, 1960, in Amritsar. He completed his schooling and graduation in Chandigarh before pursuing an MBA from IIM Bangalore.

Rajiv Sawhney began his career with Usha International, where he worked for five years and left as Deputy Divisional Manager. He then joined Jenson and Nicholson as Branch Manager before moving to Blowplast Limited, where he served as Vice President. His last corporate assignment was as CEO of Hutchinson Telecom in Indonesia, a role he held for four years.

Currently, Rajiv Sawhney heads the "*Startup Incubator Cell*" at IIM Bangalore and serves as an advisor to various companies and startups.

On January 12, 1986, Rajiv Sawhney married Kamini Sheth Saldanha in Chennai.

Kamini was born on January 6, 1964, in Madras. She studied at Good Shepherd Convent and Stella Maris College, Chennai, before completing her postgraduate degree in Mass Communication from Sophia Polytechnic, Bombay.

Kamini began her career as an Assistant News Editor at Doordarshan and, after five years, joined NDTV as the Bureau Chief in Bombay.

In 2000, Kamini took on the role of *'Anchor and Special Correspondent'* at NDTV.

A keen historian, Kamini transitioned to the arts and heritage sector in 2010, working as a *'Business Development Consultant'* at the Chhatrapati Shivaji Maharaj Vastu Sangrahalaya. In 2011, she became the Head of the *'Jehangir Nicholson Art Foundation'*, a position she held for eight years till 2019.

Currently, Kamini Sawhney is the *'Founder Director'* of 'MAP' (Museum of Art and Photography) in Bangalore, where she also serves as an Advisor and Curator.

Rajiv and Kamini Sawhney are settled in Bangalore.

SURINDER SAWHNEY and FAMILY

Kulwant Rai Sethi – Harjas Rai Sethi – Sukhanand Sethi – Ram Krishan Sethi – Dani Ditta Lal Sethi – Narsingh Das Sethi – Ganesh Das Sethi – Lakhwanti Sethi – Surinder Sawhney.

Sawhney and Malti Sawhney have three children, Ritu Sawhney, Vishal Sawhney and Ruchi Sawhney;

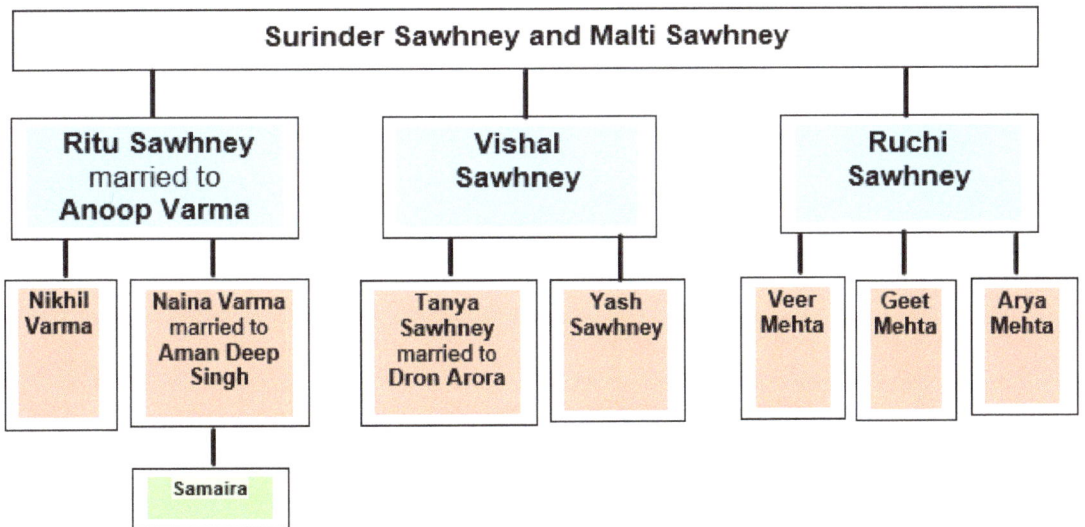

Ritu Sawhney, the eldest, was born on 9th August 1967 in Delhi. She completed her schooling at St. Mary's Convent, Kanpur, and later graduated in Home Science from Chandigarh. Ritu also specialized in Textile Designing and started her own business in textile design.

Additionally, she began organizing events under the banner *"The Great Indian Bazaar."*

On 24th September 1988, Ritu Sawhney married Anoop Varma in Chandigarh.

Anoop Varma was born on 8th January 1960 in Ambala and completed his schooling at Sr. Model School, Chandigarh.

Anoop earned a Master's degree in Economics and an MBA from Punjab University. Anoop started his career in textile exports to Japan and, since 2001 expanded into importing mechanical items from Japan. In 2007, he was appointed as an Agent for L&T in northern India.

Ritu and Anoop have two children, **Nikhil** and **Naina.**

Nikhil Varma was born on 13th July 1989 in Chandigarh. He studied at Modern School, Delhi, and later pursued a Law degree from I.P. University, Delhi. He now runs his own law firm in Delhi.

Naina Varma was born on 11th October 1993 in New Delhi. She completed her schooling at Sanskriti School, New Delhi, and graduated from Lady Shri Ram College, Delhi. She then moved to the USA and obtained a law degree from California Western School of Law, San Diego.

On 16th June 2016, Naina Varma married Aman Singh in San Francisco.

Aman Singh was born on 25th May 1989. He completed his schooling at Pittsburgh High School, California, and later graduated in Hospitality Management from Kendall College, Chicago, USA.

Aman Singh is currently the Regional Director of an aviation company in San Francisco.

Naina and Aman were blessed with a daughter, Samaira, on 21st November 2023 in Walnut Creek, California. The family is settled in San Francisco.

Vishal Sawhney was born on August 15, 1970, in Jodhpur. He studied at St. George's College, Agra, and Methodist High School, Kanpur, before pursuing Hotel Management at IHM, Lucknow. Later, he earned an MBA from Tennessee, USA, and completed a course in 'Investor Relations' at Harvard.

Vishal began his career with the Taj Group of Hotels in Goa before moving to Sterling Holiday Resorts in Ooty. After a few years, he joined the Devyani Group of Companies in Delhi, where he played a key role in establishing Pizza Hut and KFC outlets across India. Following his successful tenure with Devyani Group, Vishal moved to the USA, where he joined Apollo Chandler, a Cruise Lines Management Company, in Florida.

A few years later, he relocated to Dubai to work with Jebel Ali Hotels at Jumeirah Beach Resort.

After a brief stint in Dubai, he moved to Saudi Arabia to join the Balubaid Group, which operated in real estate and hospitality. Eventually, Vishal shifted industries and joined PVR Cinemas as their Chief Operating Officer (COO).

Having gained extensive experience, Vishal launched his own startup in 2017-18 under the brand *"14th Century"*, pioneering frozen yogurt manufacturing in India with a production facility in Gurgaon.

On November 24, 1995, Vishal married Sangita, who was born on October 9, 1973, in Delhi. Like Vishal, she also pursued Hotel Management at IHM, Lucknow. The couple later separated but share two children, **Tanya** and **Yash**.

Tanya Sawhney was born on January 14, 1997 and she completed her Master's in Architecture after schooling.

On 21st November 2023 Tanya married her school and college friend, Dron Arora at Gurgaon,

Dron Arora is also an architect. Together, they established their own architectural firm, *"Urban Design Studio"* in Gurgaon.

Yash Sawhney was born on January 12, 2000, in Delhi,

Yash pursued a specialization in Energy Law from the University of Petroleum and Energy Studies, Dehradun.

He is currently working as a Management Trainee – Law at Wipro in Gurgaon

Ruchi Sawhney, the youngest daughter of Surinder Sawhney and Malti Sawhney was born on December 5, 1973, in Jodhpur.

Ruchi Sawhney completed her schooling in Agra and later at St. Mary's Convent, Kanpur. Ruchi graduated with a Bachelor of Arts degree from Christ Church College, Kanpur University.

Ruchi's passion for hairdressing began in childhood while assisting her mother, Malti Sawhney, at her Kanpur salon, established in 1978.

After high school, she pursued a cosmetology course at YWCA alongside her degree at Christ Church College, Kanpur.

In 1995, she moved to Delhi and later advanced her skills in New York, studying aesthetics at Christine Valmy, working at Lia Schorr, and training in hairdressing with Toni and Guy and Andrew Jose.

In 1998, Ruchi Sawhney relocated to India and established her own salon, '*R's Miracle*', in Green Park, Delhi. Her exceptional talent quickly gained recognition nationwide, earning her awards such as

'*The Most Creative Stylist*' and '*Best Hairdresser*'. She was widely featured in leading magazines, including *Cosmopolitan*, *Vogue*, and *The Times of India*.

With her growing success, Ruchi moved to Gurgaon in 2015 and launched a new venture as the Founder and CEO of '*R's Just Hair*', which received numerous accolades and awards.

In 2005, Ruchi got married to Shailesh Mehta in Delhi.

The couple was blessed with a son, **Veer Mehta**, born on October 21, 2007, in Gurgaon.

Veer is finishing school at St. Xavier's, Gurgaon this year

Their twin daughters, **Geet Mehta** and **Arya Mehta**, were born on May 14, 2010, in Gurgaon and also attend St. Xavier's, School, Gurgaon, studying in grade 10th.

Ruchi Sawhney separated from her husband in 2001 and lives happily in Gurgaon with her three kids, managing the three teenager's and running her full-time salon.

VIJAY SAWHNEY and FAMILY

Kulwant Rai Sethi – Harjas Rai Sethi – Sukhanand Sethi – Ram Krishan Sethi – Dani Ditta Lal Sethi – Narsingh Das Sethi – Ganesh Das Sethi – Lakhwanti Sethi – Vijay Sawhney.

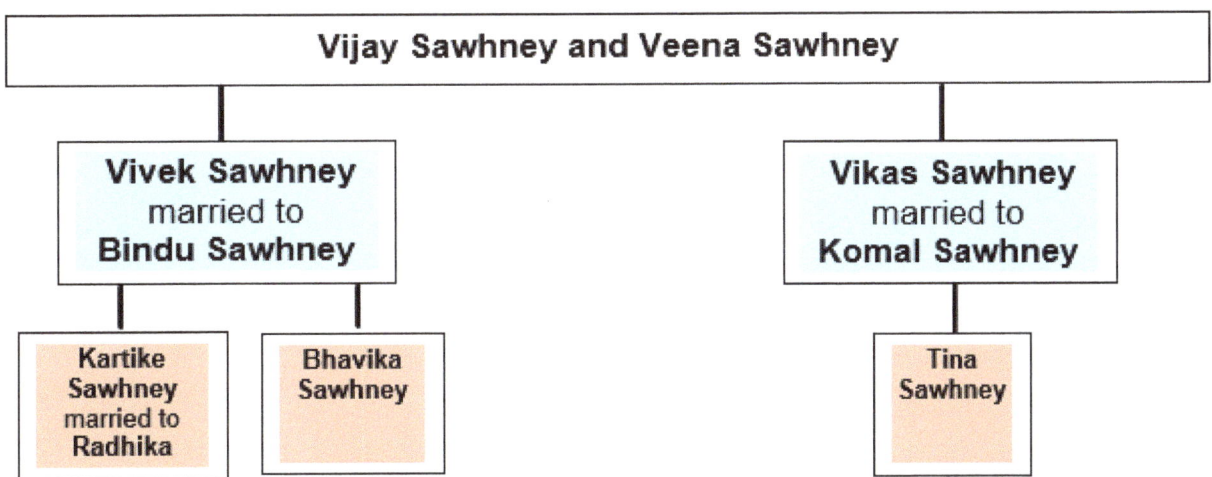

Vijay Sawhney and Veena Sawhney have two sons: Vivek Sawhney and Vikas Sawhney.

Vivek Sawhney, the elder son, was born on March 8, 1964, in Delhi. He completed his schooling at Kendriya Vidyalaya, Chandigarh, and pursued a B.E. (Mechanical) from NIT, Kurukshetra and an MBA (Marketing) from IMS Indore. He is a successful entrepreneur and owns Alliance Industries, a manufacturing unit catering to the Tea Industry.

On June 30, 1990, he married Bindu in Delhi.

Bindu Sawhney was born on November 4, 1967, in New Delhi.

She completed her schooling at Bhartiya Public School, Ambala, and graduated with a B.A. (Hons.) from GMN College, Ambala and has been a dedicated home maker.

Vivek and Bindu have two children: **Kartike** and **Bhavika**.

Kartike Sawhney was born on October 2, 1991, in Indore. He studied at Emerald Heights International, Indore and pursued an MBA in International Business from School of Economics, Indore.

Kartike Sawhney is actively involved in the family business heading Alliance International in Indore.

On June 27, 2020, he married Radhika Trehan in Dewas.

Radhika Trehan Sawhney was born on April 20, 1994, in Indore.

She studied at St. Mary's Convent, Dewas and completed her MBA from De Montfort University, Leicester, U.K.

Radhika actively participates in the family business operations.

Bhavika Sawhney was born on January 16, 1999, in Indore. She studied at Emerald Heights International, Indore and completed an MBA in Marketing from M.I.T. Ghaziabad. Currently Bhavika works as Manager, Brand Solutions at ILN Media, Gurgaon.

Vikas Sawhney, the younger son of Vijay and Veena, was born on November 30, 1967, in Delhi. He completed his schooling at Kendriya Vidyalaya, Indore, and pursued a B.E. (Mechanical) from SGSITS, Indore.

He currently serves as President at Bajaj Auto, Pune. Vikas is an expert in Robotics and has few patents to his name. On February 3, 1995, he married Komal, and has a daughter, Kareena Sawhney.

Kareena Sawhney was born on March 15, 2000, in Mumbai.

She studied at Symbiosis International School, Pune and later pursued an M.Sc. in Banking from Adam Smith Business School, Scotland, specializing in Banking.

Kareena is presently based in Mumbai working in the Financial Sector.

ASHOK SAWHNEY and FAMILY

Kulwant Rai Sethi – Harjas Rai Sethi – Sukhanand Sethi – Ram Krishan Sethi – Dani Ditta Lal Sethi – Narsingh Das Sethi – Ganesh Das Sethi – Lakhwanti Sethi – Ashok Sawhney.

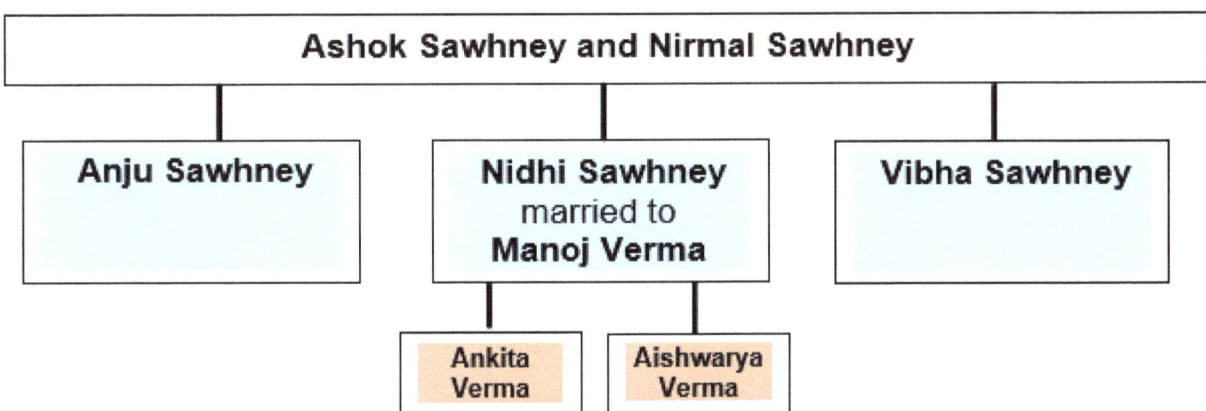

Ashok Sawhney and Nirmal Sawhney have three daughters, **Anju**, **Nidhi**, and **Vibha**.

Anju Sawhney was born on March 18, 1964, in Amritsar. She completed her schooling at St. George's, Agra, and pursued a postgraduate degree in History from St. John's College, Agra.

Anju began her career in the hospitality sector, joining the Taj Group, where she worked at various properties in Agra, Mumbai, Lucknow, and Delhi. After gaining substantial experience, she expanded her career internationally, working in Bahrain, Egypt, and the Maldives.

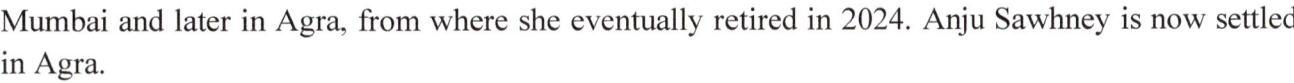

In 2011, Anju Sawhney returned to India and joined ITC Hotels, first in Mumbai and later in Agra, from where she eventually retired in 2024. Anju Sawhney is now settled in Agra.

Nidhi Sawhney was born on October 1, 1965, in Etawah, Uttar Pradesh. She completed her schooling at St. George's, Agra, and earned her graduate degree from St. John's College, Agra.

On February 24, 1996, Nidhi married Manoj Verma, who was born on January 6, 1961, in Indore.

Manoj completed his schooling in Bhopal and earned an Engineering degree from Bhopal. He worked at Bharat Heavy Electricals Ltd. (BHEL), Bhopal, and retired a few years ago.

Nidhi is currently a teacher at St. Xavier's School, Bhopal. Nidhi and Manoj have two daughters, Ankita and Aishwarya.

Ankita Vwrma was born on March 10, 1987, in Bhopal. She completed her schooling and earned an Engineering degree from Bhopal. Ankita currently works as a Plant Manager at the Madhya Pradesh Electricity Board, posted in Hoshangabad.

Aishwarya Verma was born on May 2, 1994, in Bhopal. She also completed her schooling and obtained an Engineering degree from Bhopal. Aishwarya currently resides in Bhopal.

Vibha Sawhney, the youngest daughter of Ashok and Nirmal Sawhney, was born on July 12, 1971, in Meerut.

She completed her schooling at St. Anthony's, Agra, and graduated with a B.A. degree from St. John's College in 1993.

Vibha is settled in Agra and works as a teacher at St. George's, Agra.

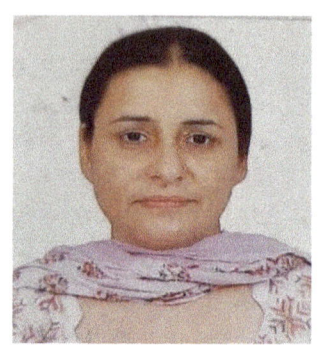

YOGI SAWHNEY and FAMILY

Kulwant Rai Sethi – Harjas Rai Sethi – Sukhanand Sethi – Ram Krishan Sethi – Dani Ditta Lal Sethi – Narsingh Das Sethi – Ganesh Das Sethi – Lakhwanti Sethi – Yogi Sawhney.

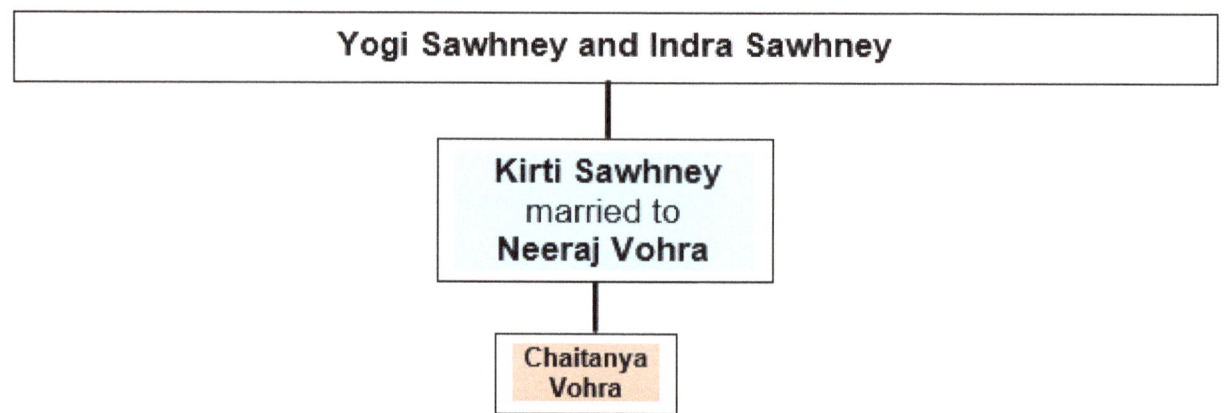

Yogi Sawhney and Indra Sawhney were blessed with a daughter, **Kirti Sawhney**, who was born on December 14, 1978, in Bangalore. She completed her schooling at Bishop Cotton School, Bangalore, and later earned a dual B.Sc. degree from Bangalore University.

With a deep interest in fabrics and fashion, Kirti pursued a course in Fashion Technology at Punjab Technical University. She began her career as a merchandiser with '*Scotic Designs*, '*Adore Apparel*s' and '*BR Knits*'. She then became the course coordinator at 'Aruna Design College' and thereafter was appointed

as the Technical Trainer for MDP and NIFT students at 'Texport Syndicate'. Alongside her professional journey, Kirti always had a passion for writing poems and stories. Embracing this interest, she launched her own YouTube channel, '*Fun with Kavita*'.

On December 2, 2009, Kirti married Neeraj Vohra in Bangalore.

Neeraj was born on February 14, 1974, in Ludhiana, where he completed his schooling before earning a degree in Textile Engineering from National Institute of Technology, Jalandhar. He has worked with

'Welspun Group' in Vapi, 'Reliance Industries' in Ahmedabad, and B.M.D. in Banswara. Currently, he serves as Vice President at 'G.M. Fabrics', based in Vapi.

Kirti and Neeraj are proud parents of their son, **Chaitanya Vohra** who was born on January 12, 2011, in Ludhiana. He is currently in the 9th grade, studying in Vapi.

KANTA SAWHNEY (AHUJA) and FAMILY

Kulwant Rai Sethi – Harjas Rai Sethi – Sukhanand Sethi – Ram Krishan Sethi – Dani Ditta Lal Sethi – Narsingh Das Sethi – Ganesh Das Sethi – Lakhwanti Sethi – Kanta Ahuja.

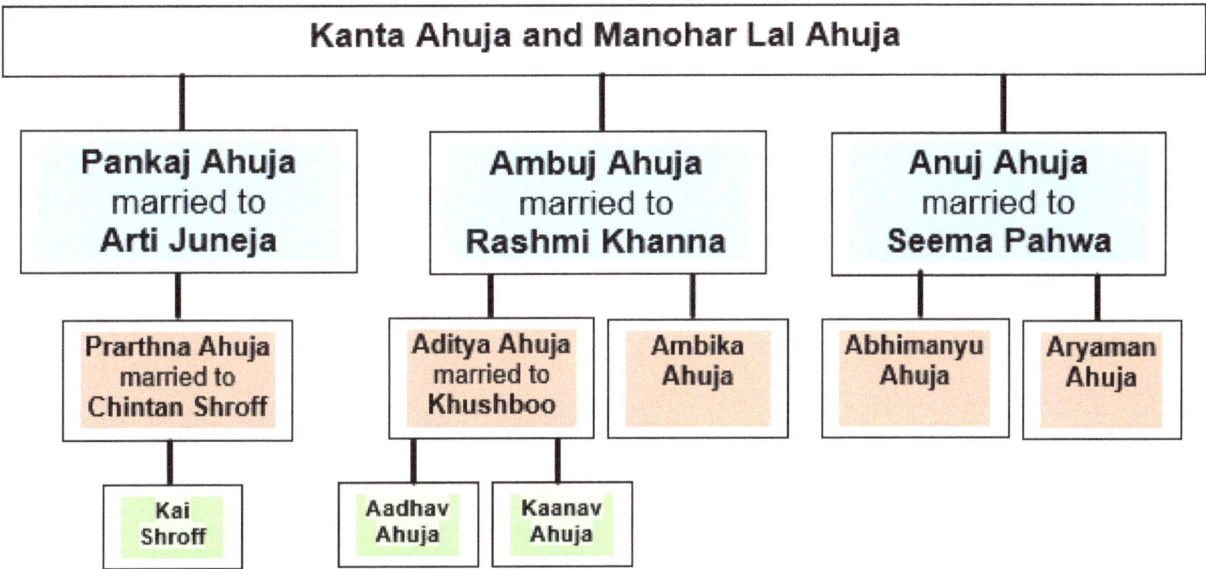

Kanta Ahuja and Manohar Lal Ahuja have three sons, **Pankaj**, **Ambuj**, and **Anuj**.

Pankaj Ahuja, the eldest of the brothers, was born on July 17, 1959, in Amritsar. He completed his schooling at BHEL School, Bhopal, and pursued a B.E. in Mechanical Engineering from SGSITS, Indore.

Pankaj began his career as a Maintenance Engineer at Tata Exports, Dewas. He later joined Engineers India Limited, Delhi, where he worked for nearly 24 years.

In 2008, Pankaj Ahuja moved to Melbourne, Australia, and joined UHDE Shedden as *Chief - Project Services*. Subsequently, he took on the role of *Team Lead Project Estimator* at Shell Global. After retiring from Shell Global he returned to India and settled in Gurgaon.

On October 19, 1983, Pankaj Ahuja married Arti Juneja in Indore.

Arti Juneja was born on December 3, 1961, in Indore. She completed her schooling at St. Raphael's School and earned a B.A. (Hons.) from Christian College, Indore. She later pursued a B.Ed. and M.A. English through Distance Learning in 1995-96. Arti began her teaching career in 1993 at Sardar Patel Vidyalaya, Delhi. In 2003-04, she transitioned into corporate training, joining *Inlingua* as a Corporate Trainer. In 2009, she moved to *CoreComm*, a Corporate Communication company based in Gurgaon, where she is presently working as an Editor.

Pankaj and Arti Ahuja were blessed with a daughter, Prarthna.

Prarthna Ahuja was born on December 7, 1985, in Indore. She completed her schooling at Sardar Patel Vidyalaya, Delhi, and pursued a degree in '*Communication Design*' in Delhi. She later obtained a Master's in '*Product Design*' from the National Institute of Design (NID), Ahmedabad.

Prarthna started her career at *Lakshya Digital* in Gurgaon before moving on to work with *Samsung* and *CISCO* in Bangalore. Currently, she is settled in Wroclaw, Poland and works as a '*User Interface Designer*' at *Ernst and Young*.

On December 16, 2012, Prarthna Ahuja married Chintan Shroff in Indore.

Chintan Shroff was born on September 19, 1985, in Mumbai. He completed his schooling at Nanavati School, Mumbai, and later pursued a degree in '*Gaming Design*' from Perth, Australia. Chintan began his career at '*Lakshya Digital*' in Gurgaon before relocating to Poland, where he worked with *Ten Square Games.* He now runs his own gaming company in Wroclaw, Poland.

Prarthna and Chintan are blessed with a three year old son, **Kai**, born on November 9, 2021 in Wroclaw, Poland.

Ambuj Ahuja was born on August 18, 1959, in Bhilai. He completed his schooling at St. Paul's School, Indore, and graduated with a B. Com degree from Govt. College for Men, Chandigarh.

Ambuj began his career as an Assistant Sales Manager at Gajra Gears, Delhi, before moving to Dunlop Tyres in the same role. After gaining significant experience, he relocated to Indore and established his own business of 'Thermal Installations.'

Following the COVID-19 pandemic, Ambuj retired. A true fighter, he has bravely endured kidney transplants and various related ailments, embracing life to the fullest.

On October 20, 1983, Ambuj married Rashmi Khanna in Indore.

Rashmi Khanna was born on April 8, 1962, at the Air Force Station, Tambaram, Chennai. Due to her father's frequent postings, she studied in multiple locations before completing her schooling at Kendriya Vidyalaya, Shillong. Rashmi earned a bachelor's degree in English Literature from GCW, Chandigarh, followed by a M.A. (English) and B.Ed. from Indore.

Rashmi Ahuja began her teaching career at Daly College, Indore. After 14 years of teaching, she was appointed Coordinator at Daly College, and in December 2009, she became Headmistress of the Junior School.

In 2018, Rashmi Ahuja received the Chief Minister's Award for Excellence in Education.

A cancer survivor, Rashmi's determination, courage, and positivity helped her overcome the disease, and she continues to serve as Headmistress at Daly College, Indore.

Ambuj and Rashmi Ahuja have two children: a son, **Aditya**, and a daughter, **Ambika**.

Aditya Ahuja was born on February 21, 1987, in Indore. He studied at Daly College, Indore, and earned an Engineering degree from M.I.T. Pune. He later pursued an MBA from Symbiosis, Pune.

Aditya started his career with Pepsi International in Moradabad and, due to his dedication and achievements, was transferred to Bangkok and later Malaysia. He currently serves as General Manager for Pepsi International – Malaysia and Philippines, based in Kuala Lumpur.

On December 6, 2021, Aditya married Khushboo, who was born on January 22, 1987, in Bihar.

Khushboo completed her schooling and college in Bangalore and later earned an MBA from Bangalore. She is currently the HR Head for Southeast Asia at GAP, based in Hong Kong.

Aditya and Khushboo Ahuja have two sons: **Aadhav Ahuja** born on December 4, 2022, in Indore, and **Kannan Ahuja** born on October 28, 2024, in Kuala Lumpur.

Ambuj and Rashmi's daughter, **Ambika Ahuja** was born on July 9, 1998, in Indore. She completed her schooling at Daly College, Indore, and pursued a triple major in Economics, Sociology, and

Psychology from Christ College, Bangalore. She later earned a Master's in Communication Sciences from the University of Amsterdam.

Ambika is currently working as a Research Analyst at *'WE ARE SOCIAL'* in Amsterdam.

Ambuj – Rashmi – Aditya – Aadhav – Ambika - Khushboo

Anuj Ahuja is the youngest son of Kanta and Manohar Lal Ahuja. He was born on April 18, 1967, in Sagar, Madhya Pradesh.

After completing his schooling at St. Paul's Higher Secondary School, Indore, he graduated with a B. Com (Hons.) and an LLB (Hons.) degree from Devi Ahilya University, Indore.

Further pursuing his education, he earned an MBA (Marketing) from Indore Management Association and a Postgraduate Diploma in International Business from the School of Economics, Indore.

Anuj Ahuja began his career as a Junior Engineer with the Madhya Pradesh Electricity Board (MPEB) and is currently serving as a Senior Accounts Officer with MPEB.

On May 18, 1994, he married Seema Pahwa in Indore.

Seema Pahwa was born on March 21, 1970, in Indore. She completed her schooling at Bal Vinay Mandir, Indore, and earned a B. Com degree from Devi Ahilya University, Indore.

Seema Ahuja is a teacher and a certified UC MAS coach specializing in Mathematics and Hindi. Additionally, she has a keen interest in garmenting and runs a business trading handmade crochet and garments.

Anuj and Seema Ahuja are proud parents of two sons, Abhimanyu and Aryaman.

Abhimanyu Ahuja was born on January 29, 1997, in Indore, Abhimanyu completed his schooling at St. Paul's Higher Secondary School, Indore. He then pursued a B. Tech in Computer Science from Medi-Caps University, Indore, followed by an M. Tech in Computer Science from Monash University, Melbourne, Australia.

Abhimanyu Ahuja started his career in 2017 with TCS in Thiruvananthapuram, Kerala. In 2018-19, he worked as a Marketing Manager at Byju's.

In 2020, Abhimanyu moved to Australia, where he is currently the General Manager at *'Glowers Renewable Energy'*, located in Sunshine Coast, Australia.

Aryaman Ahuja was born on February 24, 2002, in Indore,

He completed his schooling at St. Paul's Higher Secondary School, Indore and thereafter graduated in 2023 with a B. Tech in Computer Science from Medi-Caps University, Indore.

Aryaman Ahuja is currently working as a Business Analyst at *'Zomato'* in Indore.

BASANT SAWHNEY (KAPIL) and FAMILY

Kulwant Rai Sethi – Harjas Rai Sethi – Sukhanand Sethi – Ram Krishan Sethi – Dani Ditta Lal Sethi – Narsingh Das Sethi – Ganesh Das Sethi – Lakhwanti Sethi – Basant Kapil.

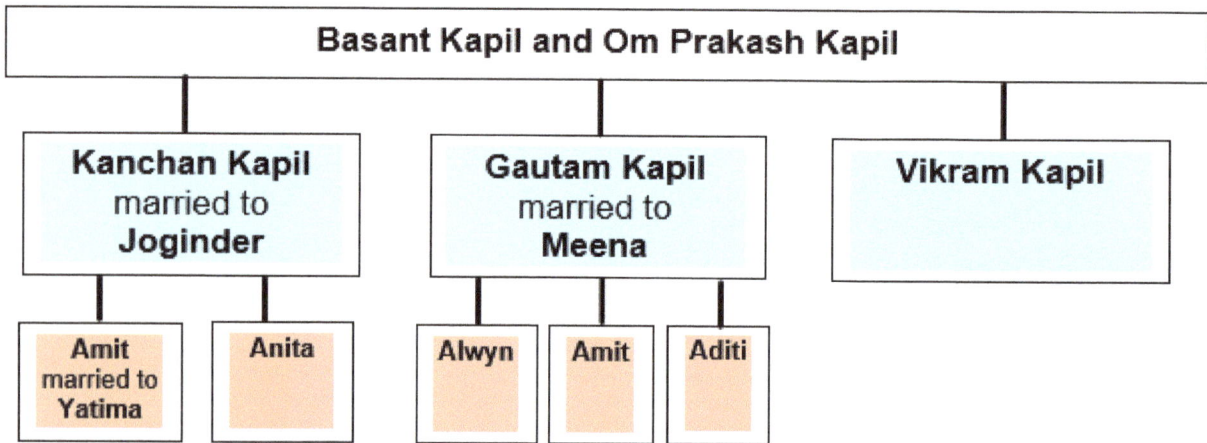

Basant Kapil and Om Prakash Kapil have three children, **Kanchan, Gautam** and **Vikram.**

Kanchan Kapil, the eldest daughter got married to Joginder and they are blessed with a son, **Amit** who is married to Yatima and a daughter, **Anita**. The family is settled in USA.

Gautam Kapil, got married to Meena and they have three children, **Alwyn**, **Amit** and a daughter, **Aditi**. The family is settled in USA.

Vikram Kapil, the youngest son of Basant and Om Prakash Kapil lives in Jallandhar.

RAJIV SETHI and FAMILY

Kulwant Rai Sethi – Harjas Rai Sethi – Sukhanand Sethi – Ram Krishan Sethi – Dani Ditta Lal Sethi – Narsingh Das Sethi – Ganesh Das Sethi – Amolak Ram Sethi – Rajiv Sethi

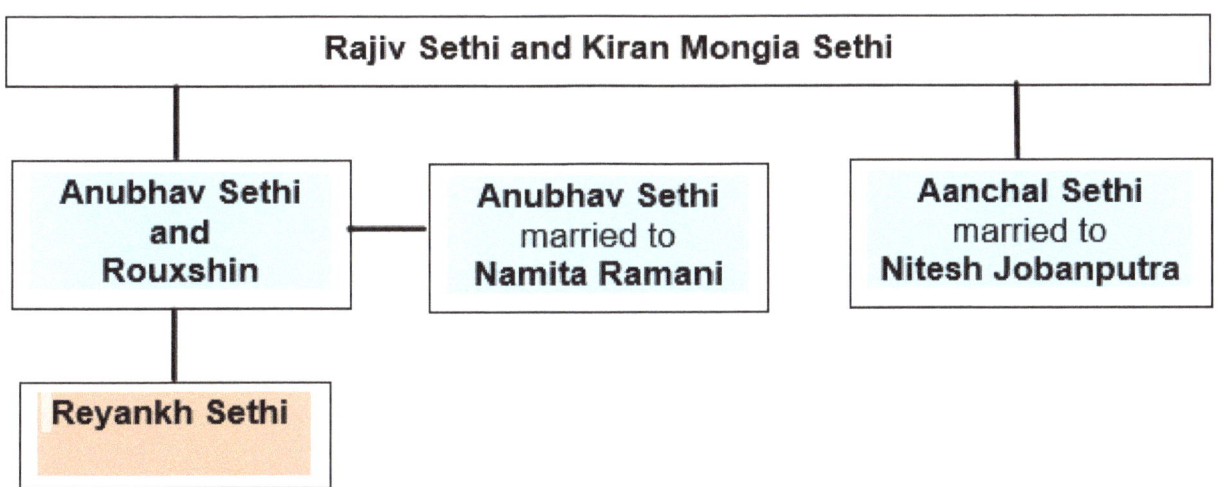

Rajiv Sethi and Kiran Sethi have two children, **Anubhav Sethi** and **Aanchal Sethi**.

Anubhav Sethi, the eldest, was born on August 24, 1979, in Kanpur. He completed his schooling at Jaipuria School, Kanpur, before pursuing a degree in Hotel Management from IHM, Mumbai, specializing as a pastry chef.

He began his career at Hyatt Regency, Delhi, before moving to Hyatt Regency, Mumbai. Following his tenure with Hyatt, he joined Leela Palace, Bangalore, as a pastry chef. After several years, he relocated to Dubai, working with Jumeirah Beach Hotel, and later joined Holiday Inn, Abu Dhabi.

To further refine his skills, Anubhav travelled to Germany and other countries for specialized training.

Currently, he serves as the Regional Head for the Middle East and India at *'Lakeland Dairies'*, a leading global dairy company, and is based in Dubai.

Anubhav married Rouxshin Vajifdar, who was also from the hospitality sector, and they had a son, **Reyankh Sethi.**

A few years after their separation, Anubhav met Namita Ramani, and they married on February 2, 2022, in Dubai.

Namita Ramani was born on January 24, 1979, in Ahmedabad, where she completed her schooling and college. She later moved to Dubai and established "*Above Digital*", a leading digital marketing agency in the UAE. She is an avid cyclist and deep-sea diver.

Anubhav is a passionate guitarist and music composer. After meeting Namita, he took up cycling, and their shared love for the sea led them to complete a deep-sea diving certification. Anubhav became a professional deep-sea diving trainer, and his adventurous spirit further led him to become a certified skydiver, completing over 350 jumps.

Their passion for adventure extended to their son, **Reyankh Sethi**, born on July 12, 2008, in Dubai, who is currently studying there.

Like his father, Reyankh has a deep love for music, guitar, cycling, deep-sea diving, and skydiving.

As a family, Anubhav, Namita, and Reyankh travel the world, pursuing their love for cycling, deep-sea diving, and skydiving.

Anubhav Sethi, Namita Ramani Sethi and Reyankh Sethi are currently settled in Dubai.

Aanchal Sethi was born on February 24, 1982, in Kanpur and currently resides in Singapore, where she works in advertising.

She spent her childhood in Kanpur and completed her 10th standard at Seth Anandram Jaipuria School in 1998. She then moved to Pune, where she pursued her H.S.C. at Symbiosis College, followed by a degree in Economics from Fergusson College.

Aanchal Sethi later earned a Master's Degree in Development Communication from the Mass Communication Research Institute at Jamia Millia Islamia, Delhi.

Since leaving home in 1998, Aanchal has lived, studied, and worked in multiple cities and countries, including Pune, Mumbai, Delhi, Ahmedabad, Dubai, Greece, and Singapore.

Her career has been deeply rooted in advertising, and she has worked with leading global agencies such as Lintas, Rediffusion, DDB, Iris Worldwide, and Ogilvy.

Driven by curiosity and creativity, Aanchal has cultivated a deep love for art and music.

Anchal Sethi is passionate about traveling and has explored over 32 countries, often embarking on solo journeys.

Beyond her professional and travel pursuits, Aanchal has a strong interest in alternative healing and meditation.

Her dedication to these fields has led her to become a Reiki master, a certified clinical hypnotherapist, and an art therapy practitioner.

On 9th December 2022, Aanchal Sethi married Nitesh Jobanputra. Born on March 30, 1978, in London,

Nitesh Jobanputra works in project management within the banking industry.

Aanchal's journey continues to be one of exploration, creativity, and personal growth, embodying a spirit of adventure and lifelong learning.

Both Aanchal Sethi and Nitesh Jobanputra along with their pet '*Chai*' are settled in Singapore.

Kulwant Rai Sethi – Harjas Rai Sethi – Sukhanand Sethi – Ram Krishan Sethi – Dani Ditta Lal Sethi – Narsingh Das Sethi – Ganesh Das Sethi – Amolak Ram Sethi – Poonam Sethi

POONAM SETHI and FAMILY

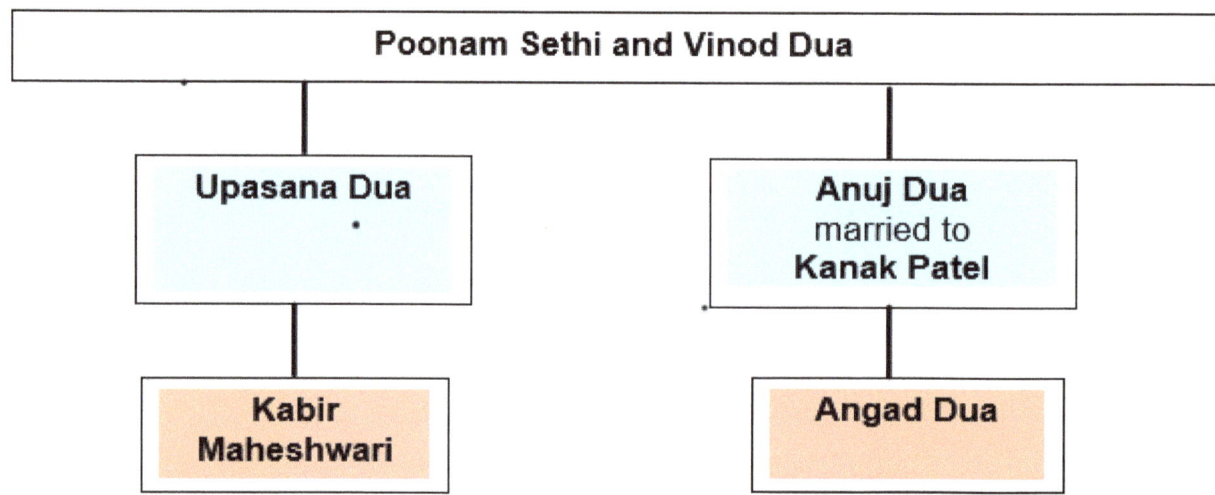

Poonam Sethi and Maj. Vinod Dua have two children, Upasana Dua and Anuj Dua.

Upasana was born to Poonam and Vinod Dua on September 19, 1977, in Binaguri, West Bengal. She completed much of her schooling in Delhi, attending both Loreto Convent School and Delhi Public School, before pursuing a B.A. Honours degree in Economics.

After working for a year with Dr. Mallika Sarabhai in Ahmedabad, Upasana went on to complete her Postgraduate degree in Social Communication Media from Sophia Polytechnic in Mumbai.

Upasana has been married twice and has a son, **Kabir Maheshwari**, from her first marriage. Kabir, born on December 8, 2003, is currently studying a double major in Economics and Informatics at the University of Washington, Seattle.

Upasana began her career in the development sector and has since worked in advertising and marketing across the Asia Pacific region, including nearly a decade spent in Indonesia. She is now based in India, where she serves as the Executive Director of Strategy for the APAC region at the design consultancy Landor.

Anuj Dua was born on February 11, 1980, in Kanpur and raised in New Delhi, where he completed his schooling at St. Columba's School. He then pursued an undergraduate degree in Architecture from Institute of Environmental Design Anand before immigrating to the United States to attend the University of California, Los Angeles (UCLA) for a master's program in Architecture.

A member of the American Institute of Architects, Anuj has designed buildings across the United States and Canada, including performing arts venues, industrial and retail spaces, restaurants, and both affordable and market-rate multifamily housing.

His award-winning work focuses on sustainable architecture, and he has completed several pioneering projects, such as one of California's first Zero Net Energy, Energy Star, and LEED-certified affordable housing projects.

On December 10, 2008, Anuj married his college sweetheart, Kanak Patel, in New Delhi.

Kanak, born on April 21, 1980, in New Delhi, is an interior designer based in Los Angeles, CA. Kanak holds a bachelor's degree in interior design and a master's degree in industrial design from Arizona State University.

Anuj and Kanak are blessed with a son, **Angad. Angad Dua** was born on October 8, 2019, in Los Angeles.

Anuj, Kanak and Angad are settled in Los Angeles, CA, with their Labrador, Izzy.

Kulwant Rai Sethi – Harjas Rai Sethi – Sukhanand Sethi – Ram Krishan Sethi – Dani Ditta Lal Sethi – Narsingh Das Sethi – Ganesh Das Sethi – Amolak Ram Sethi – Rajat Sethi

RAJAT SETHI and FAMILY

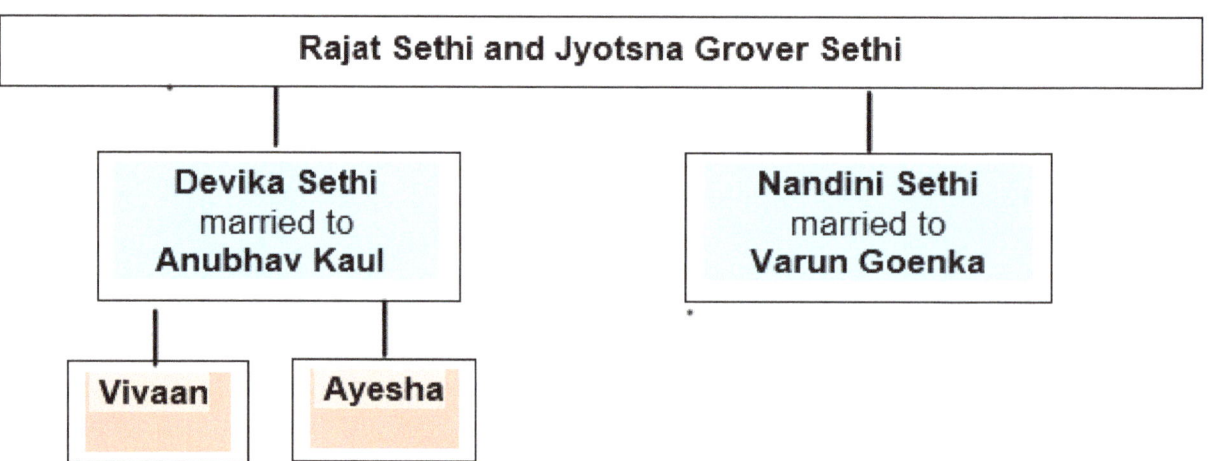

Rajat Sethi and Jyotsna Grover Sethi have two daughters, **Devika Sethi** and **Nandini Sethi**

Devika Sethi was born on April 21, 1987, in Chennai. She completed her schooling at Air Force Bal Bharti School, Delhi, from 1992 to 2005 and pursued her undergraduate studies at St. Xavier's College, Mumbai, from 2005 to 2008. She later went on to earn her higher education degree from INSEAD, France, from 2014 to 2015.

After returning to India, Devika began her professional career as a Consultant with McKinsey in Mumbai. She later transitioned to Private Equity and is currently an Equities Investor at a Hedge Fund in Singapore.

On November 10, 2011, Devika married Anubhav Kaul in New Delhi. Anubhav was born on February 20, 1982, in Bhubaneswar. He is a Career Fund Manager at an Investment Management Firm in Singapore.

Devika Sethi Kaul and Anubhav Kaul are blessed with two children, Vivaan and Ayesha

Their elder son, **Vivaan Sethi Kaul,** was born on April 2, 2017, in Hong Kong, followed by their daughter, **Aisha Sethi Kaul**, who was born on February 7, 2020, in Hong Kong.

Both children are currently attending school in Singapore, where the family is happily settled.

Nandini Sethi was born on May 28, 1990, in Bombay. Shortly after, her family moved to Delhi, where she completed most of her schooling. After the 10th grade, she attended Woodstock, a boarding school in Mussoorie, for high school. She then pursued her undergraduate studies at St. Xavier's College, Mumbai, graduating with a double honour's degree in Sociology and Anthropology.

Dedicated to the nonprofit sector, Nandini focused her career on promoting educational equity in India. In 2019, she moved to Hong Kong to pursue a Master's in Nonprofit Management, graduating with Distinction.

She continues to work in the nonprofit sector in Hong Kong.

On November 24, 2023, Nandini married Varun Goenka in Hong Kong, where they continue to reside.

Varun was born on May 12, 1989, in Bombay. He completed his schooling at The Cathedral and John Connon School and earned his undergraduate degree from Mumbai University. He later pursued a Master's in Sports Management at London Metropolitan University, graduating with Distinction.

With over a decade of experience in Sports Management, Varun relocated to Hong Kong in February 2024. He currently works in Event Management playing football and other sports on weekends.

www.ingramcontent.com/pod-product-compliance
Ingram Content Group UK Ltd.
Pitfield, Milton Keynes, MK11 3LW, UK
UKHW060214240426
12048UKWH00031BB/1726